The Search for Winchester's Anglo-Saxon Minsters

The Search for
WINCHESTER'S
Anglo-Saxon
MINSTERS

Martin Biddle

with illustrations by
Simon Hayfield

Oxford
2018

Winchester's earliest Anglo-Saxon church (later known as Old Minster) as it may have looked about 650, looking south-east.

The Anglo-Saxon Old Minster in its final form, completed 992–4, looking north-east, with the west front of New Minster, built 901–3, and its tower built in the 980s in the background.

In memory of
Birthe Kjølbye-Biddle
1941–2010

Birthe Kjølbye-Biddle was a Danish archaeologist who transformed approaches to archaeological excavation in England.

Joining the Winchester excavations as a student from the University of Aarhus in 1964 she introduced metric measurements and imposed new standards of rigour in excavation, stratigraphic recording and analysis, which were adopted throughout the work of the Winchester Excavations Committee. This technical brilliance provided the basis for her forthcoming posthumous publication on the archaeology of the Anglo-Saxon minsters (Winchester Studies 4.i). The present book is a tribute to Birthe by Simon Hayfield, whom she selected as the principal illustator of WS 4.i, and whom she trained in archaeological illustration.

Published by the Winchester Excavations Committee

© Winchester Excavations Committee 2018
Registered Charity No. 210455

The moral rights of the author and illustrator have been asserted

First edition published in 2018

All rights reserved. No part of this publication may be reproduced, stored in a retrieval system, or transmitted, in any form or by any means, without the prior permission in writing of the Winchester Excavations Committee, or as expressly permitted by law, by licence or under terms agreed with the appropriate reprographics rights organization

You must not circulate this work in any other form
and you must impose this same condition on an acquirer

All paintings and drawings are by Simon Hayfield unless otherwise stated.

Photographs by A. R. Smith (p. 10), R. C. Anderson (pp. 11, 15–16 (lower), 18, 22–23 (lower), 31 (upper left), 38, 48–9 (left), 65), M. Biddle (pp. 12, 16 (upper)), E. Cloutman (pp. 13, 68, 70), T. Slade (pp. 19, 23 (upper), 31 (bottom)), J. W. Fletcher (pp. 20–21, 25 (lower)), J. W. Hopkins III (p. 24), John Crook (p. 34), C. Chapman (p. 71), G. Worman (back cover).

All photographs and illustrations including those by Simon Hayfield are the copyright of the Winchester Excavations Committee unless otherwise stated.

Published in United Kingdom by Archaeopress Publishing
www.archaeopress.com

ISBN 978 1 78491 857 6
ISBN e-pdf 978 1 78491 858 3

Typesetting in Garamond and Futura by Clare Chapman

Book design by Simon Hayfield and Clare Chapman

Editing by Clare Chapman and Katherine Barclay

Copy-editing by Robert Peberdy

Front cover images (clockwise from top left): The Anglo-Saxon Old Minster c.650; Old Minster with New Minster in the background c.992–4; excavation on the Cathedral Green 1969; Anglo-Saxon wall painting; and excavation of the chalk foundations of the north apse of Swithun's martyrium at Old Minster c.975

Contents

viii   Acknowledgments

ix   Preface

1   Introduction

2   Anglo-Saxon Winchester

10   Archaeological excavations and finds

32   Understanding the evidence

44   Evolution of Old Minster

60   Destruction of Old Minster

66   The Royal Quarter

70   Winchester Studies

74   Further Reading

Acknowledgements

The Winchester Excavations Committee acknowledges with gratitude the generous support it has received over the years in conducting the excavations and preparing the results for publication. The search for the minsters was begun by Roger Quirk CB (d. 1964), whose articles on the Old and New Minsters led directly to the excavation of the site of the proposed Wessex Hotel in 1961 and thus to the establishment in 1962 of the Winchester Excavations Committee, under whose aegis the results described in this book were achieved.

The excavation of the Old and New Minsters in 1961–70 was accomplished by students from over thirty countries, especially from the the University of North Carolina at Chapel Hill, North Carolina State and Duke University in the United States, supervised by many from this country who have since made their name in archaeology. Directed over successive seasons by Birthe Kjølbye-Biddle and Martin Biddle, the excavations and team of volunteers made it possible to rewrite a whole chapter in the history of English architecture and archaeology.

The work could never have been undertaken without the enthusiastic support of successive Deans of Winchester Cathedral, notably Oswin Gibbs-Smith and Michael Stancliffe whose terms of office coincided with the excavations alongside their cathedral.

The Winchester Excavations Committee is grateful to its many financial supporters without whose generous help over many years the work of the Committee and its publications could not have continued. The Committee wishes to thank in particular Andante Travels, the Avocet Charitable Trust, Dame Mary and Captain Christopher Fagan, the Friends of Winchester Studies, Richard Greaves, Philip Gwyn, the Hampshire County Council, the Hampshire Cultural Trust, the Hampshire Field Club, the Headley Trust, Damon de Laszlo, the Linbury Trust, David Lloyd, the Marc Fitch Fund, Nigel McNair Scott, Rupert Nabarro, Julia Sandison, †Chris Webb, the Winchester Archaeology and Local History Group (WARG), and the Winchester City Council for their most recent and invaluable support.

The Winchester Excavations Committee wishes also to acknowledge with gratitude the following individuals who have contributed to the making of this book: Katherine Barclay, Clare Chapman, Beatrice Clayre, Tony Hill, Francis M. Morris, Neil Pafford and Robert Peberdy.

Preface

Over the forty-eight years since our excavations north of the cathedral came to an end in the late summer of 1970, work on the analysis and writing up of the results has been in progress, but in fits and starts as other projects and other responsibilities have intervened, in England, but also in Jerusalem and in Coptic Egypt. These have all influenced our growing comprehension of both the archaeology and the architectural history of Winchester's minsters, and also of the immensely complex interpretation of the records made during the excavations of 1961–70.

When Birthe Kjølbye-Biddle died on 10 January 2010, the text of Volume 4.i of Winchester Studies, *The Anglo-Saxon Minsters of Winchester*, and the drawings and other illustrations needed to accompany the text, were all but finished, but much remained still to be completed by way of editing and cross-checking. A great deal of this has now been done but there is still a considerable amount of revision and updating required before the book will be ready for publication.

Birthe published a long series of articles on various aspects of the excavation and its interpretation in the intervening years, while directing the production of the drawings required for the final publication. Simon Hayfield was recruited as illustrator of the volume in 1975 and almost all the hundreds of drawings in the final publication – plans, sections, drawings of objects, diagrams, and other illustrations – are his work. During this time Birthe and I also gave many lectures on the emerging results, both in England and abroad, usually to colleagues but also, and most especially in Winchester, for members of a wider public. We had not however until now, although several efforts were made, produced a book designed for this wider audience. It is entirely due to the initiative of our artist and friend Simon Hayfield that the present book has come into being. His work is most evocatively summed up on pp. 58–9 in his three-dimensional view of Old Minster as completed in the early 990s – an astonishing achievement.

Martin Biddle

Director of the Winchester Research Unit
February 2018

Introduction

On 14 October 1066 a traveller approaching Winchester from the east, little knowing how events that day at Hastings were to change what he saw, would have looked down from St Giles's Hill over an ancient walled city. With suburbs spreading outside each of the five gates, the regular streets within – laid out by King Alfred or by his father or one of his older brothers nearly two centuries before – were lined with houses, mostly wooden, a few perhaps of stone. At the traveller's feet in the south-east quarter of the city lay the royal and ecclesiastical quarter, with the palaces of king and bishop, and three great monasteries: Old Minster, the cathedral church, founded over four centuries before, containing burials of kings of Wessex, England, and Denmark; New Minster, founded in 901–3, the burial church of Alfred and his house; and Nunnaminster, a house for women, founded by Ealhswith, Alfred's widow, at about the same time.

Following the Norman Conquest and over the course of the next 75 years or so, the city of Winchester was transformed. Old Minster was demolished in 1093–4, after the dedication beside it of the eastern parts of the new Norman cathedral. New Minster was demolished in 1110, following the move of its community to a new abbey in the northern suburb of Hyde. Nunnaminster was rebuilt on its old site but on a vast scale.

William the Conqueror built a great hall on land taken from New Minster adjacent to the site of the Anglo-Saxon royal palace in the centre of the city, and threw up the earthworks of a vast castle to the south of West Gate on the highest ground within the walls.

Over time, the locations of both the Old and New Minsters were lost. And they remained lost, until quite by chance a programme of excavation was set in motion in 1961 that was to transform our understanding of the history and archaeology of Winchester and revolutionise the archaeology of towns.

Anglo-Saxon Winchester

Winchester (*Venta Belgarum*, 'market or 'place' of the Belgae) is a town of Roman origin: it was the fifth largest of twenty or so urban places in the province *Britannia*. Its defences were first built of earth and timber about AD 70, enclosing an area of 58 hectares with four or possibly five gates. A grid of gravelled streets was laid out about the same time: a principal street running between the west and east gates, with two west–east streets laid out to each side of the main street and six north–south streets, together defining 39 rectangular city blocks (*insulae*). A vast forum, measuring 110 by 100 metres, was built in a central block by about AD 100, the largest single building in Winchester before the second half of the twentieth century, excepting only the Norman cathedral. Nothing is yet known of other public buildings such as the baths, although an aqueduct bringing water from perhaps 28 kilometres up the valley presumably supplied both the baths and other buildings. By the later second and third centuries there were several temples and many houses, some with mosaic pavements. A stone wall was added to the defences about AD 300 and bastions were added to the outer face of the wall perhaps 50 years later.

By the later fourth century Christianity was widespread in Britannia, with perhaps as many as twenty bishops with their churches inside the by then four provincial capitals and in the fifteen or so local capitals such as Winchester. A Romano-British church has not yet been found in Winchester, but a few objects show that Christianity was not unknown. A century later, the invasions of pagan Germanic peoples, the Angles, the Saxons, and the Jutes (who later, together with the surviving British population, became known as the English), had brought organised life in towns to an end. Christianity survived only in the north and in the far west (including Ireland), partly as the result of fifth-century missionary activity associated with the name of St Patrick, and in an enclave of British survival north-west of London, around the Roman city of *Verulamium*, the burial-place of St Alban.

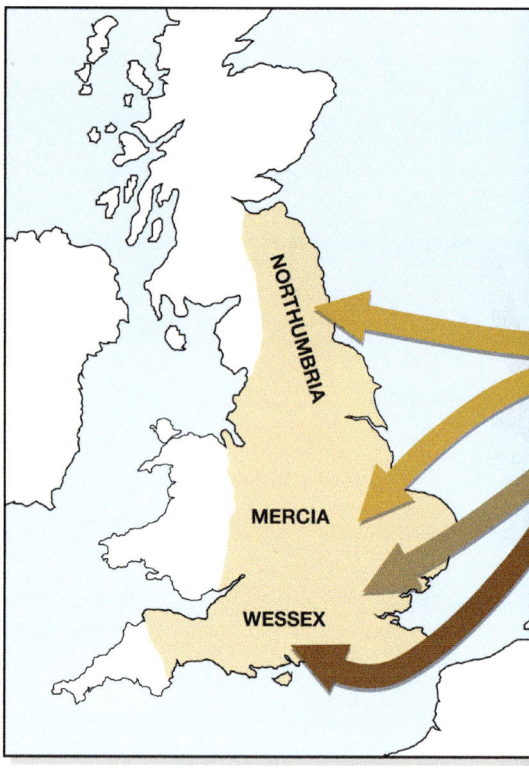

Roman Britain had long successfully resisted attacks on its eastern shores – its so-called litus Saxonicum *– from across the North Sea. The collapse of Roman power meant that from the early 5th century onwards these attacks were increasingly successful, allowing the Angles, the Saxons, and the Jutes to establish pagan kingdoms in what had been the Roman provinces of Britannia.*

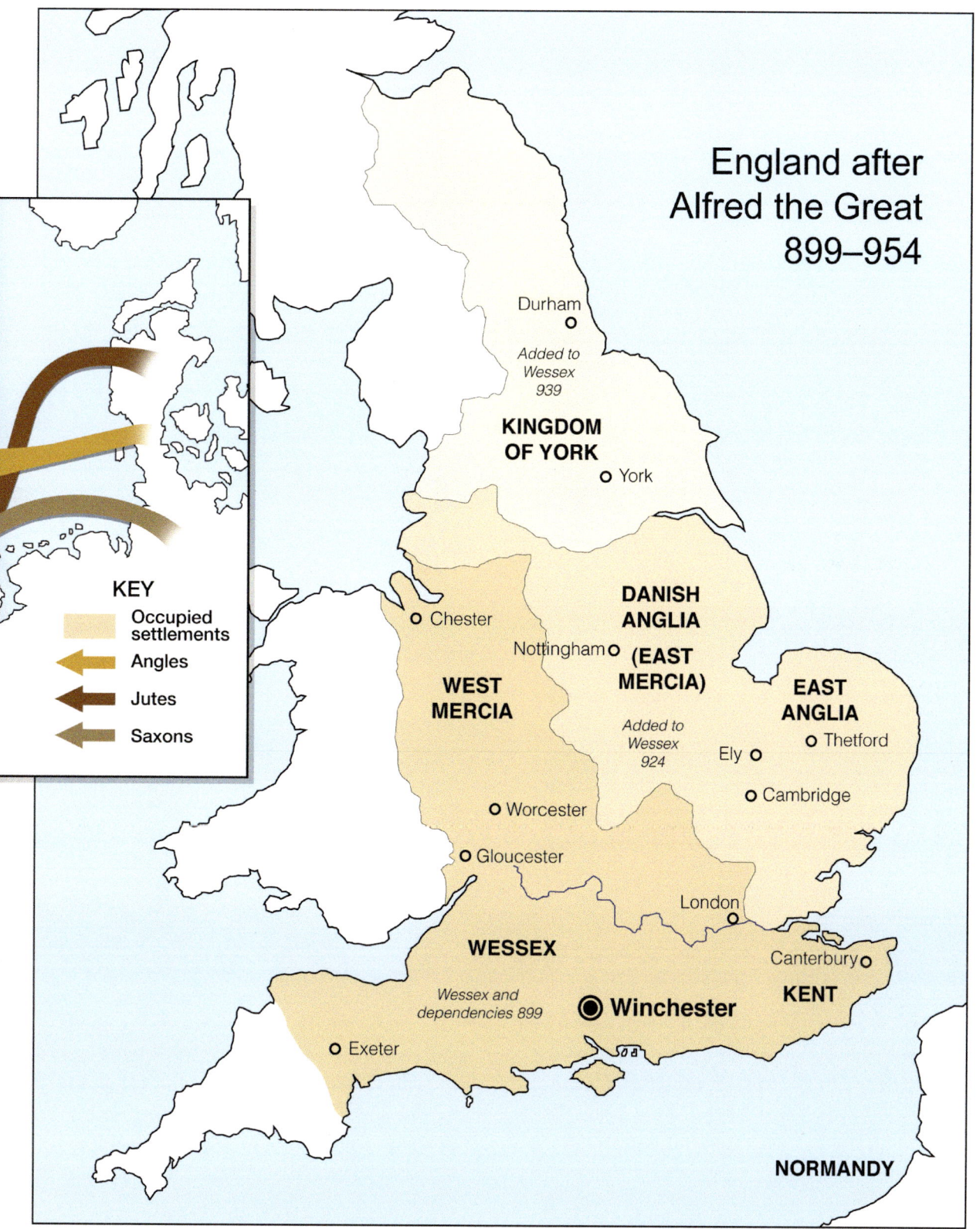

By the 7th century Roman Britain had become a patchwork of Anglo-Saxon kingdoms, principally Northumbria, Mercia, East Anglia, Kent and Wessex. From the late 8th century these kingdoms came under Scandinavian 'Viking' attacks. By Alfred's time the kingdom of York, half of Mercia, and East Anglia were under Scandinavian rule. Wessex under Alfred survived and by 954 its kings had become rulers of a united kingdom of England.

Anglo-Saxon Winchester

From the fifth century onwards several Anglo-Saxon kingdoms came into being and as a result of the mission of St Augustine from Rome in 597 gradually became Christian. These kingdoms were frequently at war, but gradually the Northumbrians in the north, the Mercians in the centre, and the West Saxons in the south, each with their own royal dynasty, came to dominate. In the ninth century Viking raids and subsequent large-scale Scandinavian settlement in the east of Britain nearly resulted in the Danes taking over the whole country, but the eventual success in battle of Alfred, the king the West Saxons, and his successors led to the emergence of Wessex as the dominant English power.

Shortly after 630 a priest whose name has come down to us as Birinus (in reality, perhaps Virinus) was sent from Rome by Pope Honorius I (625–38) to continue the conversion of the Anglo-Saxons begun by Augustine in 597. Birinus reached the region of the Upper Thames in the early 630s, baptised King Cynegils of Wessex at Dorchester-on-Thames in 635, and was bishop there until his death in 649 or 650. The tradition is that Birinus founded a church at Dorchester, but nothing is yet known of its architectural character.

King Cenwalh of Wessex (ruled 642–72) built a church at Winchester but the date of its construction is not recorded, although a church dedicated to St Peter and St Paul was presumably in existence by 660 when Wine, the first bishop of Winchester, was appointed. Its plan and the methods employed in its building suggest it was built while members of Birinus's mission were still alive and this may indicate that Old Minster, as this church later became known, was founded around or not long after his death in 649 or 650, a date broadly confirmed by the generations of burials which soon began to surround the church. By Alfred's time Winchester was certainly the principal place of royal burial: of the 27 English rulers before the Norman Conquest whose place of burial is known, ten were laid to rest in Winchester, and no more than three in any one other place.

(top) Portrait of King Alfred of Wessex (871–99) wearing a diadem in the Roman manner on a silver penny minted in the later 870s. Found in the excavation of Old Minster in 1964.

(bottom) The first coin to bear the name of Winchester, abbreviated to PIN, Old English for WIN, minted in the city in the later years of King Alfred. London BM 1959, 1210.23 (© The Trustees of the British Museum; both images twice life-size)

(right) Alfred in bronze, as the heroic warrior king by Hamo Thornycroft, erected in 1901, dominates the east end of The Broadway between Abbey House, official residence of the Mayor of Winchester, to the south, and the chapel and hall of St John's Hospital to the north.

Kings of Wessex and England, 802–1100

Ecgberht, king of Wessex, 802–39

Æthelwulf, 839–58 (nominal from 855)

Æthelbald, 855–60

Æthelberht, 860–5

Æthelred I, 865–71

Alfred the Great, 871–99

Edward the Elder, 899–924

Æthelstan, king of England, 924–39

Edmund, 939–46

Eadred, 946–55

Eadwig, 955–9

Edgar, 959–75

Edward the Martyr, 975–8

Æthelred II the ill-advised, 978/9–1016

Swein Forkbeard, 1013–14 (brief conquest)

Edmund Ironside, 1016

Cnut, 1016–35

Harold Harefoot, 1035–40

Harthacnut, 1040–2

Edward the Confessor, 1042–66

Harold II, 1066

Edgar Ætheling, 1066

William the Conqueror, 1066–87

William II Rufus, 1087–1100

Anglo-Saxon Winchester

From Roman *Venta* to Saxon *Wintanceaster* and the creation of the Anglo-Saxon street pattern

Shortly after AD 400 the forum and streets of Roman Winchester became disused and were then gradually lost. Little is known of what happened for the next two centuries but there are hints in the surrounding countryside that the former Roman city remained a focus of authority and it was probably to serve this that a Christian church was founded about 650 in the centre of the walled area, immediately south of the site of the Roman forum. About two centuries later, in or shortly after the time of Swithun as bishop of Winchester (852–63), or in the reign of Alfred or one of his older brothers, the area inside the former Roman walls was laid out with an entirely new grid of streets. These were arranged to serve the commercial role of High Street, with back streets parallel to north and south providing easy access for goods, and with eighteen north–south streets to provide for a growing population.

Over succeeding centuries the frontages along the new streets of Anglo-Saxon Winchester were divided up, into large blocks of property allotted to one or other of the so-called 'seven great fiefs'. Nothing is recorded of this process, but it is precisely defined by the 'ownership' of the individual tenements forming each block of properties, as recorded in the two surveys preserved in the 'Winton Domesday'.

Late Saxon Winchester

(above) Late Saxon Winchester. The regular pattern of the streets, still mostly in use today, was laid out in the later 9th century, possibly in the reign of King Alfred, within the line of the Roman city wall. The precincts of the three minsters, Old Minster, New Minster, and Nunnaminster, and the sites of the royal and bishop's palaces, occupy the whole south-eastern quarter of the walled area, a setting of royal and ecclesiastical power unparalleled in Anglo-Saxon England.

(left) By the 10th century the north–south streets of the new Anglo-Saxon planned town were becoming fully built up, with densely packed houses, some parallel to the street, others at right angles, and with small churches to serve the needs of the new parishes placed as here on the street and provided with a small eastern apse.

Anglo-Saxon Winchester

Swithun, bishop of Winchester (852–63)

(right) The imperial abbey of Corvey (North Rhine-Westphalia, Germany) looking east at the exterior of the westwork built 873–85. Although the towers and uppermost gallery were added in the mid-12th century, Corvey gives a good idea of how the westwork of Old Minster might have looked (built 975–80 over the site of St Swithun's grave, see pp. 50–1) (Courtesy of Westfälisches Museum für Archäologie, Münster)

(left) St Swithun, 18th bishop of Winchester (852–63), shown in golden episcopal vestments as a saint giving a blessing. Illustration in The Benedictional of St Æthelwold, painted 971–84. London BL, Add. MS. 49598, f. 97v. (© The British Library Board)

Swithun was bishop of Winchester from 852 to 863 at a time when the Vikings were raiding Wessex. There is some evidence that he played an important role in formulating and executing the ecclesiastical policies of King Æthelwulf of Wessex (839–58) and that his competence in Latin was above that of some of his fellow bishops. A poem written after Swithun's death in 863, possibly based on an inscription, says that he built a stone bridge at the East Gate of Winchester.

This is all we know for certain of Swithun's life. Later tradition claimed that he defended the city against Viking attack. Whether that is true or not, he was buried in a highly prominent position immediately outside Old Minster, between the west door of the church and the tower of St Martin, and his tomb was marked by a stone cross. As we shall see, archaeological evidence confirms the position of Swithun's original grave. It also shows that at the time of his burial the area between the church and St Martin's tower was otherwise free of graves, and that the closeness of the grave to the west door would have compelled those entering to pass to one side or the other. Here are clear indications of the special importance accorded to the burial of Swithun in 863.

In the time of Bishop Æthelwold (963–84), if not earlier, Swithun came to be recognised as a saint. His grave was opened in 971 and his remains were placed in a golden shrine at the high altar of the church. The site of his burial became the focus of an immense 'martyrium', which was later reconstructed as a westwork (see Corvey, this page and below, pp. 48–51).

Archaeological excavations and finds

The search for the sites of the Old and New Minsters

By the end of the Middle Ages nobody knew where the Old Minster church had stood. The monks seemed to believe it lay on the site of the present Norman cathedral. As recently as the late 1950s, it was still possible to argue that it lay either north or south of the present nave, to the north of the choir or indeed beneath the present cathedral where parts of it were thought still to be seen in some rough masonry visible in the crypt.

Equal uncertainty surrounded the site of the New Minster church. In 1959 it was still supposed that it might lie to the east of Morley College on the site of the then Cathedral Car Park, where in 1961 Trust Houses Ltd were about to start building what is now the Wessex Hotel. There was no legal requirement in those days for archaeological excavation of an urban site, however important it might seem to be. Roger Quirk, educated at Winchester College and then a senior figure in the Department of Education and Science, had for some years in his spare time been studying Latin sources for Winchester's minsters and had just published the first modern study of Old Minster. This involved discussion of the possible site of New Minster, the most likely site of which appeared to be the Cathedral Car Park.

Moving fast, Quirk secured the support of Trust Houses Ltd, Winchester's City Council, the Society of Antiquaries, and the Ministry of Works, and an excavation was arranged by the City Council. The Society of Antiquaries, when

Looking east from the air at the excavations in August 1966 on the site of Old Minster alongside the nave of the present cathedral. The trenches are laid out on the alignment of Old Minster which differed slightly from that of the Norman cathedral.

asked to recommend someone to direct the work, suggested the present writer then in his final year at Cambridge.

Excavation showed that the car park was not, as supposed, the site of the New Minster church founded by King Edward the Elder in 901–3, but rather of one of the minster's domestic buildings, probably the residence of Abbot Riwallon (1072–88), formerly prior of Mont Saint-Michel in Normandy and the most important of the abbots of New Minster before its removal to Hyde in 1110. But the dig led early in 1962 to the foundation of the Winchester Excavations Committee, which for the next decade carried out excavations across the city on a scale never before attempted in any English city. The first two years of the Committee's work led to the discovery of the churches of both the Old and New Minsters.

The former royal and ecclesiastical quarter of the walled city of Anglo-Saxon and Norman Winchester looking east from the air in 1969. The site of the Anglo-Saxon and Norman royal palace lies in the foreground, bounded by the curving line of Little Minster Street. Alongside the nave and west end of the cathedral, archaeological excavation is in progress on the site of the Anglo-Saxon cathedral known as Old Minster, with the site of New Minster immediately to the north. The Nunnaminster, founded by Alfred's queen, Ealhswith, lies beyond, under the Guildhall and Abbey House and its gardens. In the top right-hand corner, the line of the Roman and medieval city wall encloses the bishop's palace dominated by the ruins of the residence built by Bishops Giffard and Henry de Blois in the 12th century.

Archaeological excavations and finds

(above) The first excavations took place in 1961 at the former Cathedral Car Park in advance of the construction of the Wessex Hotel. It was thought that this might actually be the site of the New Minster church, founded by Edward the Elder in 901–3. This proved not to be the case but the site revealed the west range of the Roman forum flanked by one of the main north–south streets of the Roman city and the courtyard of a Roman house whose well is visible in the foreground. Later buildings included an oval (twin-apsed) Anglo-Saxon chapel (perhaps the lost church of St Michael), and the residence probably built by Abbot Riwallon of New Minster in 1072–88.

(right) In 1970 the last excavation north of the cathedral returned to the problems of the domestic buildings of New Minster. A range of buildings running from west to east across the eastern part of the Cathedral Green, just to the north of the north transept of the cathedral (seen in the background), was found to be the south range of a cloister, probably the infirmary of the 10th-century New Minster. After the Norman Conquest, when New Minster lost the western part of its precinct for the construction of William the Conqueror's palace, the monks appear to have rebuilt the former infirmary as their principal cloister and to have occupied it until they left their home for a new site outside the walls at Hyde in 1110. The discovery of their refectory beside the north transept of the cathedral provides stark evidence of just how crowded the monastic sites had become by the early 12th century.

Archaeological excavations and finds

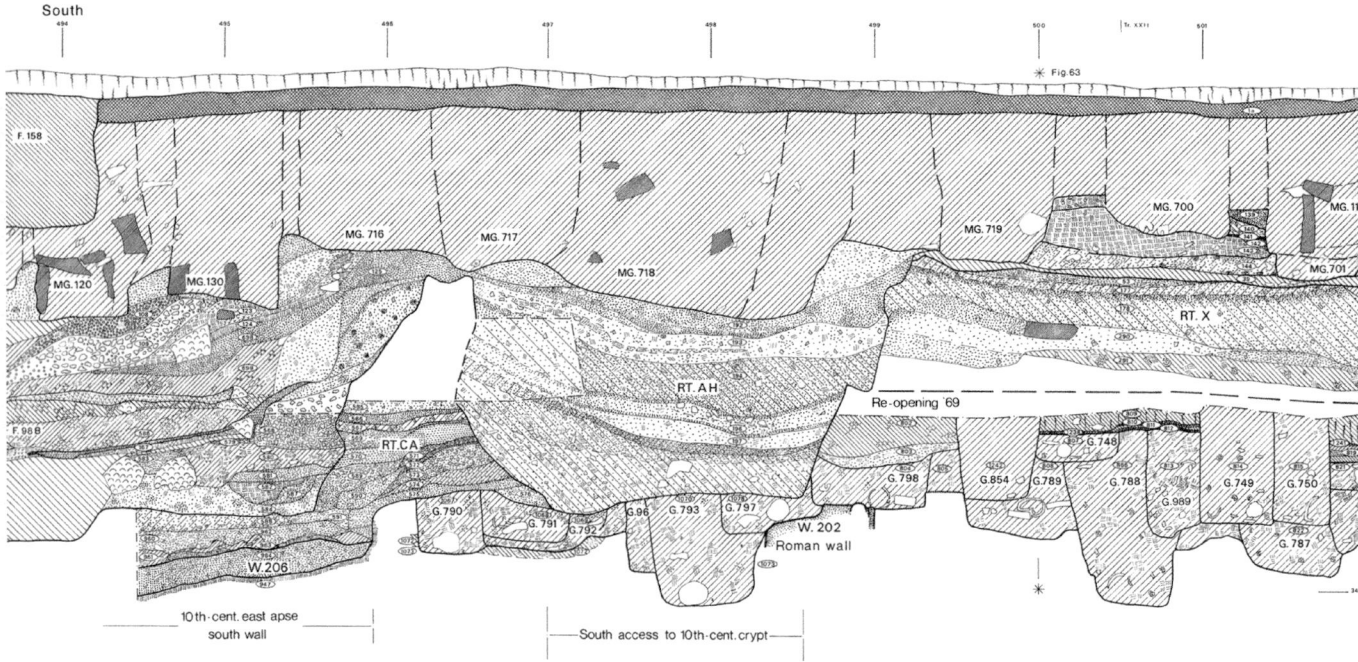

Since it was known from written sources that the churches of the Old and New Minsters had lain so close together, such 'that a man could scarcely make his way between them', it followed that the discovery of one would lead rapidly to the other. The most likely site of Old Minster seemed to be to the north of the nave of the present cathedral, so it was there that three small trenches were dug in the summer of 1962.

A trench half way along the north side of the nave revealed in three weeks a remarkable sequence. Under a deep layer of medieval burials was a metre-thick layer of rubble derived from a large building of flint and mortar construction, apparently of two periods. The later period was represented by a mortar floor which lapped a stone coffin, showing that the two were contemporary in setting. The earlier period, also represented by a mortar floor, sealed a pit into which a massive block of oolitic limestone had been set, with a large roughly circular cutting on its upper surface. The walls by contrast were represented only by the 'robber-trenches' left behind by the workmen demolishing the building. Although the precise significance of these features could not be known from a single small trench, it was clear that they formed part of a major ecclesiastical building earlier than the present cathedral, a church which could only be identified as Old Minster.

(right) The excavation of the west end of the 7th-century Old Minster seen from above, looking north. Three periods of construction are visible. The two parallel walls running diagonally out of the picture to the upper right, with a red tessellated floor between them, are part of a Roman public building added to the south side of the forum in the later 2nd or early 3rd century AD. They are cut through by a foundation of broken red Roman tiles and flints forming a right angle. This represents the west front and north wall of the 7th-century Old Minster built in part of material recycled from demolished Roman buildings. To the left, the white chalk is part of the foundation of the martyrium erected over the burial place of St Swithun after 971, at the point where this was added to, and therefore butted up against, the north-west corner of the 7th-century church.

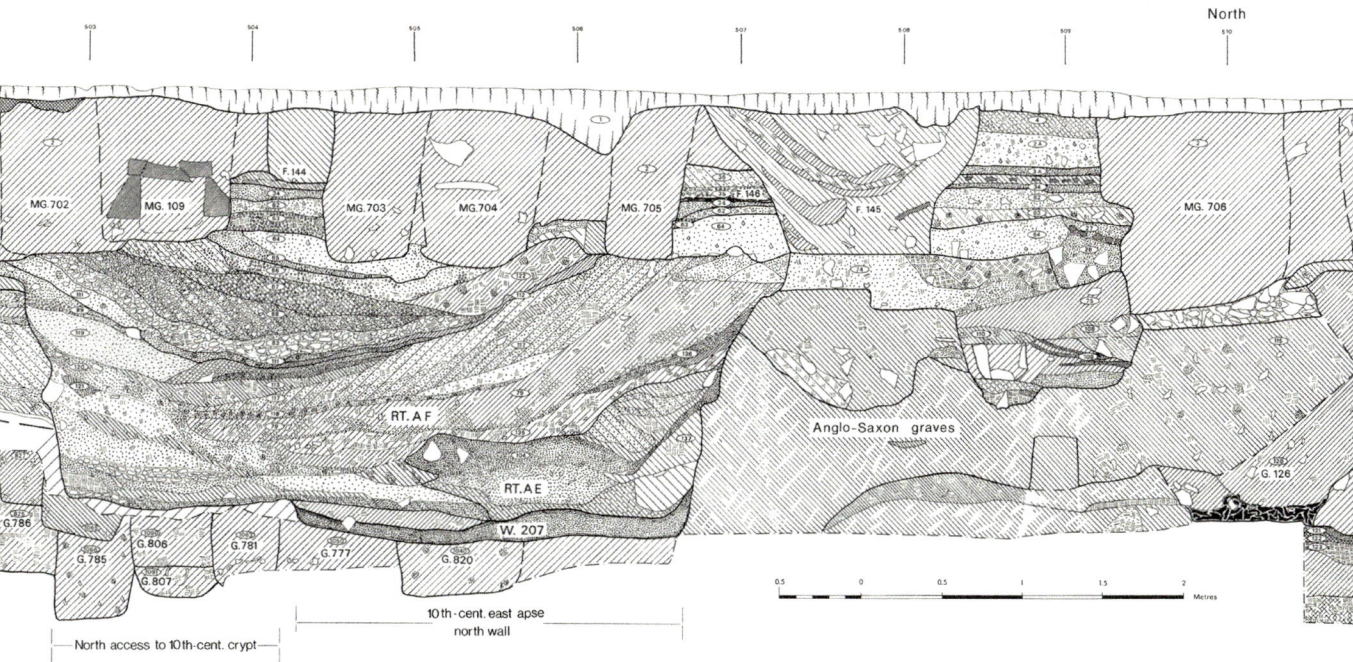

(above) This is an example of part of an archaeological section drawn for publication from many 'field' drawings made to scale on site during the course of the excavation. It runs from south (left) to north and covers a distance of 18 metres across the east end of Old Minster as reconstructed and extended in the years between 980 and 992–4. The deeper narrow 'pits' across the bottom of the drawing show graves dug before the extension of the east end was first laid out in 980. The larger 'sweeps' of layers above the graves are deposits of rubble and other features indicating the lines of debris surviving from the demolition of the north and south walls of the east end of Old Minster. The deeper narrow pits above represent graves in the public cemetery which had grown up over the site of the demolished Old Minster from about 1200 to the end of burial in this area, about 1540.

Archaeological excavations and finds

Full excavation in later seasons showed that by extraordinary chance this first trench had found the base of the altar of the original Old Minster church of about 650 and that the empty stone coffin which lay beside and above the altar in the second phase is probably to be identified as the coffin in which Swithun was buried in 863, moved here from the site of his original burial to the west of the minster. A more remarkable discovery is scarcely to be imagined.

The following summer the trench was extended 30 metres to the north across what turned out to be the nave of the New Minster church, its south wall lying, as recorded, so close to the north wall of Old Minster that one could scarcely walk between them. With both churches identified, a decision had to be taken about how to proceed.

It was decided to excavate Old Minster first, as far as possible in its entirety, and to leave New Minster, apart from the south and north walls

of its nave and its relationship to Old Minster, for a later campaign. In the event New Minster remains essentially unexcavated to this day.

Excavation in long narrow trenches is one thing. To plan and carry out the excavation of a whole vast building, and to record the evidence as fully as possible as it is removed and destroyed in the process of excavation itself, are quite a different matter. How this was done, how the evidence was recorded, and how the results are interpreted are something else again.

The following pages portary the progress of the digging and some of the finds that were discovered. The photograph below left and its caption give some idea of the excavation of the Norman monument of around 1110 marking the grave of St Swithun, and of the medieval monument of around 1200, as drawn on this page (right).

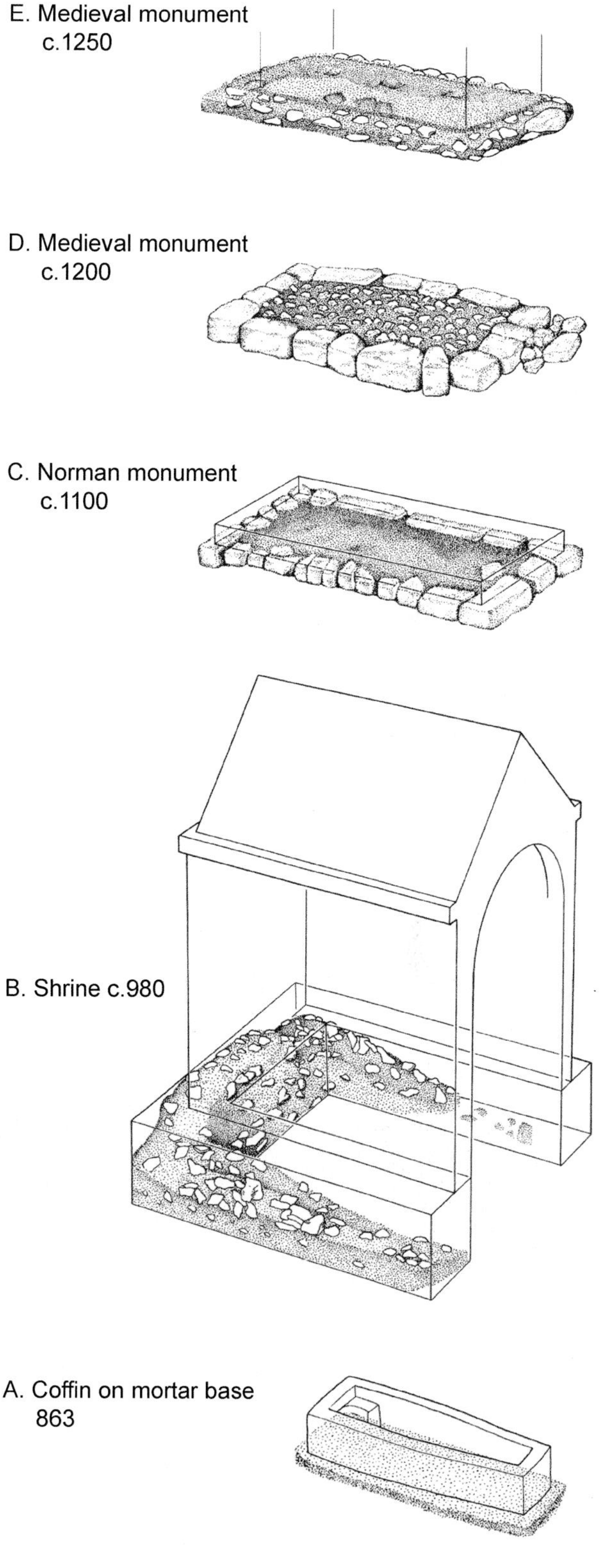

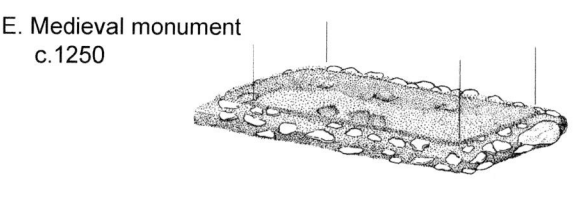

E. Medieval monument c.1250

D. Medieval monument c.1200

C. Norman monument c.1100

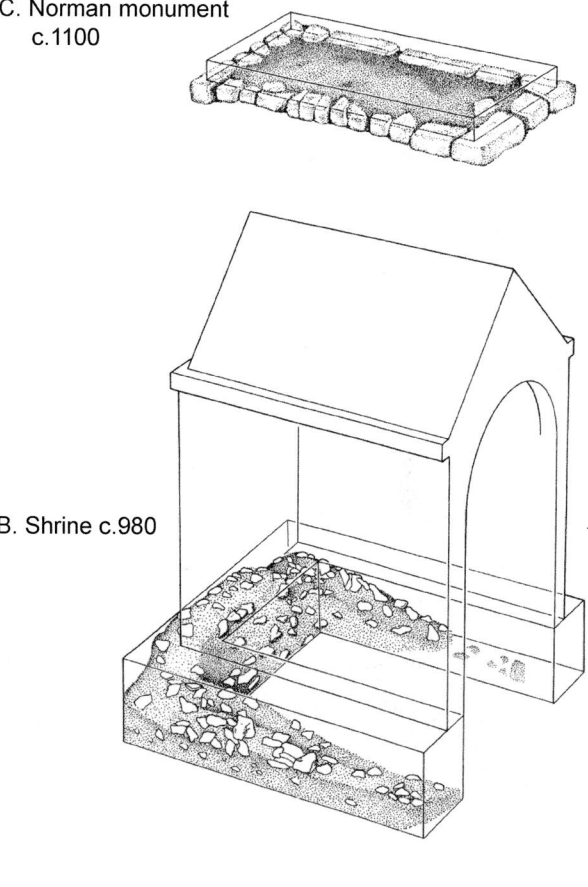

B. Shrine c.980

A. Coffin on mortar base 863

(above left) A trench dug in 1962 on the suspected (but then still unknown) site of Old Minster revealed what we now know is the base of the altar of the 7th-century church at the point where it was overlain by an empty stone coffin, now realised to have been the coffin in which Swithun was buried outside the front of the church in 863. Excavations in 1963–9 set this discovery in the context of the development of the minster over four centuries from c.650 to 1093 (see pp. 42–59).

(left) The mortared stone base, looking south-east, of about 1200 (compare D to right) of a monument in the chapel outside the north door of the cathedral nave. This monument marked the exact site and alignment of St Swithun's original burial place (compare the photographs on pp. 20–1). The pink plaster surface of the 'memorial court' laid out over the site of the westwork of Old Minster, on which the first monument was precisely positioned, can be seen passing beneath the edges of the later bases (compare the photograph on p. 21).

(right) 'Exploded views', looking north-west, of the evidence for the burial place of Swithun and the sequence of monuments marking the site of his burial from 863 to the end of the Middle Ages.

Archaeological excavations and finds

The mortared flint walls of the small rectangular building in the foreground are all that remain of the shrine built around the site of St Swithun's original burial place after the discovery and removal of the stone coffin containing his body in 971 (see p. 17, illustration B). The massive foundations of rammed white chalk formed part of the vast memorial building built in 971–5 around the site of the saint's original grave (see pp. 42–3, 48–9). The flint wall below the scale is the south wall of the memorial chapel built over the demolished minster but around the site of the saint's grave in the 1200s (see p. 20).

In 863 St Swithun was buried in this stone coffin outside the west door of the minster. In 971 his body was taken up, 'translated', to lie in a new shrine on the high altar, and the coffin in which he had originally been buried was moved inside the church and probably placed beside the altar. When the new east end of Old Minster was completed and dedicated in the early 990s the coffin was slightly raised up and placed as here to lie beside the steps leading up to the new high altar (see 1b on illustration on pp. 58–9), visible to all who came to the church. Hollows worn in the sides of the coffin show where the faithful were able to reach inside and touch the place where the saint had once lain (see p. 22, upper stone coffin). When the minster was demolished in 1093–4, the coffin was left in position, although the steps up to the altar and the stone slabs of the floor were removed for reuse.

Archaeological excavations and finds

Excavation in 1966 uncovered the remains of St Swithun's Chapel outside the door (just visible here to the right) in the north wall of the cathedral nave. The earlier, much larger chapel and its later smaller successor had both been reduced to the top of their foundations when demolished in the 16th century shortly after the Reformation. The foundations of the monument over the exact site of St Swithun's grave can be seen inside the smaller walled rectangle towards the top of the picture.

Following the demolition of Old Minster in 1093–4, the site of the Anglo-Saxon westwork was covered with a layer of pink plaster in which some of the coffined graves originally within the westwork were preserved in position. The area was presumably intended to preserve the location and retain the memory of certain important persons whose bodies were left in position and not moved into the new cathedral. This 'memorial court' was focused on the precise site of the grave of Swithun, which was now marked out in the pink plaster surface by a low stone monument (C in the sequence on p. 17).

The memorial court was gradually abandoned and became covered by part of the cathedral cemetery, graves being cut down through the pink plaster as the photograph on this page shows. But the monument over Swithun's grave was several times restored (photograph below, and D and E in the sequence on p. 17) and in the thirteenth century a stone chapel was built around it. In the fifteenth century the chapel, by then reduced in size, could be reached from the cathedral by a door (photo opposite) in the north wall of the nave. St Swithun's chapel was finally demolished, presumably at the Reformation, and was lost until excavated in 1967–8.

As excavation proceeded it became clear that before the earlier chapel was built, the exact site and alignment of the saint's original grave had been preserved by a stone setting around which a surface of a pink plaster had been laid. When this plaster was removed, it was found to have been laid over the site of the westwork built around the saint's original grave in 971–80 but demolished in 1093–4.

Archaeological excavations and finds

Burials

For over four centuries, from the later seventh to the end of the eleventh century, Old Minster was the principal burial place in Winchester, with graves surrounding the church on all sides. Very few people were buried inside the building before the later tenth century, and then only those of the highest rank in church and society. There were also many burials around New Minster and in its nave, but not to the south where the two churches lay only a metre apart. In both churches the royal burials lay in the east end.

Monolithic stone coffins

Seven monolithic stone coffins were found, but they seem not to have been used in Winchester before the ninth century. Each was carved in a single block of stone, sometimes with a niche and 'pillow' to receive the head. Many also had holes in the base for drainage (as shown in the upper coffin above right). Some examples are more tapered towards the foot with thinner sides (as shown in the lower coffin above right).

Iron-bound wooden coffins

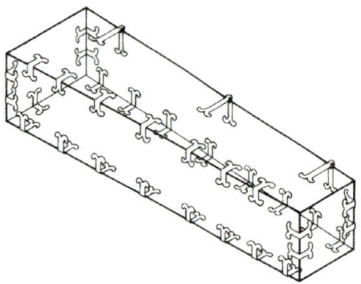

There were 22 wooden coffins discovered in the excavations bound with sometimes elaborate ironwork held fast by nails with tinned (i.e. silvered) heads. Remarkably, at least four of these iron-bound coffins had lids hinged along one side with iron straps, and one even had a lock. Magnificent objects, comparable to the iron-bound doors of churches, these coffins make one wonder whether they were domestic chests made with the expectation that one day they would hold the body of their owner.

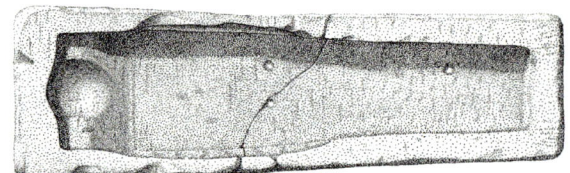

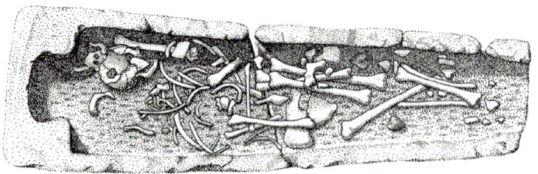

(above) The upper coffin, in which Bishop Swithun was thought to have been buried in 863 (Grave 71, see also pp. 16–17), is perhaps the earliest example we have of a monolithic stone coffin from Winchester. The sides at shoulder level were worn smooth by the hands of pilgrims after 971 when the coffin was moved into the church. The lower coffin (Grave 125) lay tight against the outside of the great east apse of 992–4 and contained the body of a young adult male.

(far left and left) The iron bound coffin shown here comes from a burial of the mid 9th century (Grave 821). It is the earliest and most elaborate with 35 fittings. The burial lay up against the outside of the south wall of the original 7th-century church, a position of great significance at a time when burials were not permitted inside the church itself. The photograph shows the excavation of the grave with the iron fittings as found in position around the skeleton of an adult male. The grave was also exceptionally deep, and when excavated was close to the present water table, hence the water visible in the photograph.

Gold braids

Five of the Old Minster burials had the remains of gold thread embroideries around the head. The longest, seen here, was a braid 1.6 cm wide woven with threads of spun gold from a cloth originally perhaps 60 cm in length. This lay around the head of a male of 21–25 buried in Grave 67 inside Old Minster in the mid to late ninth century. A young male buried inside the church is unlikely at this date to have been a senior ecclesiastic and was probably a member of the Wessex royal family (for the silver garter hooks found at his knees, see p. 30).

(above) The right side of the skull from Grave 67 with surviving spun-gold threads from perhaps three woven braids found attached to the skull.

Charnel

(left) The huge quantity of human bones deposited in the rectangular hole left after the Norman builders of the new cathedral had removed the foundations of the westwork of the Anglo-Saxon Old Minster.

During the building of the Norman cathedral, graves in the huge cemetery along the south side of Old Minster were dug up to make way for the foundations of the new church. The bigger bones, skulls, and arm and leg bones were collected and those belonging to over 1,000 individuals were reburied in the vast hole from which the stone foundations of the westwork of Old Minster had been 'robbed'. The skulls, as seen here, were properly laid in neat order to the west, as in the graves from which they came, but the 'long' bones were thrown in haphazardly until the whole bottom of the 'robber-trench' was covered to a depth of over half a metre with 'charnel'. Most of the smaller bones were missing, presumably because it was not thought necessary to collect them. The bones were then covered with earth and lost to sight until discovered in 1969.

Archaeological excavations and finds

Grave markers

Nearly one thousand graves of men, women, and children were excavated in and around the Old and New Minsters in 1962–9. Some of these were perhaps unmarked but others clearly had markers at the head or foot of the grave or perhaps both. These could have been made of wood or stone. However, only stone markers were found during the excavations, perhaps because wooden ones did not survive. Some graves may also have been covered by a stone slab which might be inscribed, like that of Gunni shown here.

Grave 119 is the only grave that provides the name of the person buried. Gunni, a man of 45 or more, was buried in the 1020s or 1030s outside the east apse of Old Minster. His Norse name and title were cut in Anglo-Saxon letters and language down the centre-line of his elegantly shaped gravestone.

All we know of Gunni comes from the inscription, which reads in Old English: + HER LID GVNNI, EORLES FEOLAGA, 'Here lies Gunni, the Earl's companion'. 'Eorl' might be the rare personal name 'Eorl', in which case Gunni would have been 'Eorl's companion'. If, as seems probable, it refers to a person with the rank of 'earl', the most likely here in Winchester would be Earl Godwin of Wessex who died in Winchester on 15 April 1053 and was himself buried in Old Minster.

Of the twelve footstones found, some, such as the stone at the foot of Gunni's grave (above left) and fragments from two others, show the Hand of God coming down from Heaven holding the Cross, a sure promise of Resurrection. Two further fragments offer the same promise, one showing what is perhaps Golgotha, with crosses on a hill, and the other, which is perhaps the most striking (above right), seems to show an image of the Tomb of Christ with the curtains pulled aside to show a lamp hanging over the place of Christ's burial and resurrection, a sign of the expectation of eternal life. It is thought to have been carved locally in the 10th century.

Decoration

Painting and plaster

The foundations and walls of the Anglo-Saxon Old Minster were built of flints and rubble reused ('robbed') from the ruins of Roman buildings, dressed inside and out with plaster, some of which contained red dust from powdered Roman tiles. New stone, mainly oolite limestone from the Bath region, was used for architectural details and decorative sculpture. Although thousands of fragments of broken wall-plaster were found in the excavations, only a very few of these were painted, suggesting that wall decoration was perhaps provided by woven textiles or painted hangings (see pp. 56–7).

Almost all of the broken fragments of wall-plaster found were plain or bore traces of whitewash. There were two exceptions: a few pieces of pink plaster which were given their colour from an admixture of ground-up Roman tile, seen here on the left, and a very few pieces of painted plaster, of which the fragment on the right is the only piece of any size. The pink plaster, nicknamed 'SOMP' on site (Saxon Old Minster Plaster), seems to have been intended to be relatively waterproof. It was used principally on the outside of the great western façade added to the nave of Old Minster in the earlier 10th century as a response to the building of New Minster in 901–3 (see p. 47).

The largest fragment of wall-painting found came not from Old Minster but from the foundations of the south wall of the New Minster nave, where it had been reused as rubble from some earlier building demolished when New Minster was built in 901–3. This was possibly the monasteriolum, the 'little monastery' built by King Alfred for the scholar-priest Grimbald from St Bertin in Normandy (see p. 66). Dating from the later 9th century, it is a unique survival of Anglo-Saxon painted decoration. Paintings in Anglo-Saxon manuscripts suggest that it probably shows part of three or four figures from a 'heavenly choir' in the Carolingian style.

Archaeological excavations and finds

Sculpture

Over 90 fragments of sculpture were found in the excavation of Old Minster, almost all carved in oolitic limestone from the Bath region. A few pieces were still intact, such as the tomb stone of Gunni and the head- and foot-stones illustrated above (see p. 24), but most of the fragments were small and clearly trimmed from larger blocks which had been removed to provide stone for building the new Norman cathedral. Enough survive, however, to show that Old Minster had been elaborately decorated with carved stone pillars with capitals and bases, and with running patterns of simple and sometimes complicated interlace, the bands of which were typically patterned with lines of pellets. Others were decorated with acanthus leaves and other plants. There were twisted 'cabled' mouldings, elaborate floral patterns, some on a large scale, and human and animal figures, as on the

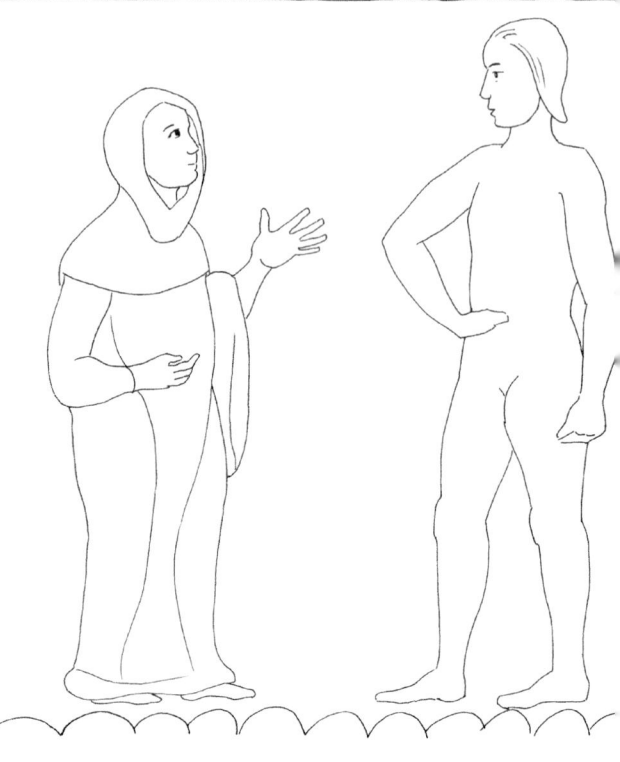

(left) The 'Sigmund' stone is part of a larger carved scene which seems to represent an episode from the Saga of the Volsungs, perhaps celebrating the shared history of England and Denmark. Drawing by Frances Rankine.

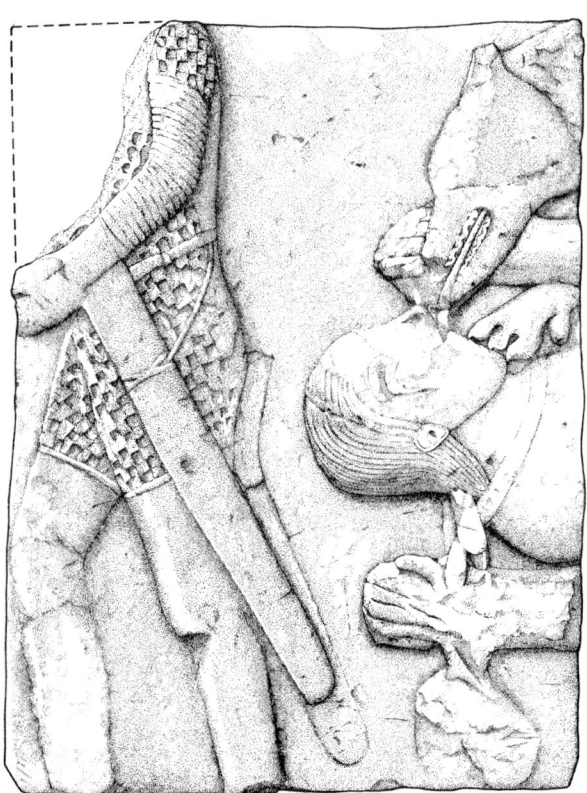

'Sigmund' stone on this page evidenced usually only by small pieces. Paint has not survived on these fragments, either because it was washed away during burial, or because the effect was mainly provided by strong relief.

Although only tiny fragments usually survived, exceptionally there was one complete block measuring 69.5 by 52 cm with a thickness of 27 cm, which was found in the eastern apse. It shows parts of two scenes. To the left a man wearing chain-mail with his hand on a sword walks to the left into a scene, the rest of which is lost. To the right another man lies on the ground, his hands raised. He is bound around the neck, perhaps to a stake in the ground. On top of him is a canine – the dew-claw is clearly *(above) This interpretative diagram shows the narrative scene, as it might have looked, with Sigmund's sister and trusted servant to the left and the rest of Sigmund and the wolf, and the stocks, to the right. Drawing by Frances Rankine.*

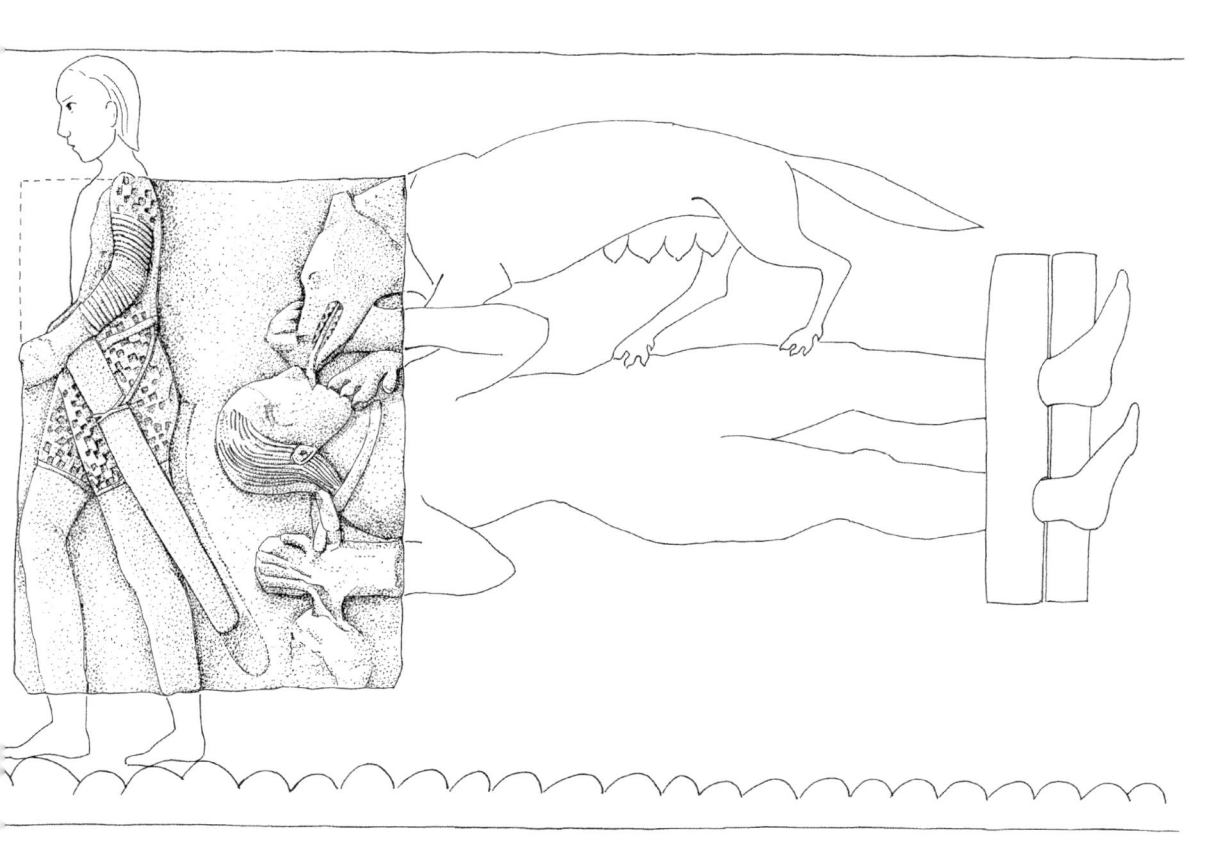

shown – its mouth open but not biting and its tongue extended into the man's mouth. Clearly more stones are needed above, below and to either side to complete the story. However, the stone seems to display an episode from the Saga of the Volsungs where Sigmund, like his nine brothers before him on nine successive nights, is tied up in a wood to die. As on the previous nights, a she-wolf comes to kill him. But Sigmund's sister (as the interpretative diagram suggests) has sent her trusted man to smear honey on Sigmund's face and in his mouth. The wolf comes, licks Sigmund's face, and thrusts her tongue into his mouth. Sigmund bites down and tears out the wolf's tongue. In her death agonies, the wolf breaks the stocks in which Sigmund is held.

This scene seems to be part of an immense frieze, closely comparable in general arrangement to the Bayeux Tapestry, perhaps 25 metres or more in length, which celebrated the shared genealogy and traditions of the kings of Wessex and Denmark. This was probably positioned around the interior of the apse, in a building which was to become the principal church and burial place of the dynasty established by the marriage of the Danish Cnut to the English Emma, widow of Æthelred, king of England. Harthacnut, their son, was buried there in 1042, and Emma herself in 1052, by which time Edward, her son by her first marriage to Æthelred, was king. The last royal burial in Old Minster was that of Richard, second son of William the Conqueror, who died about 1075 while hunting in the New Forest.

Archaeological excavations and finds

Floor tiles

In the very first trench cut across Old Minster in 1962 a few fragments of multi-coloured glazed tiles were found, the different colours separated by raised ribs. Nothing like them had been found before anywhere in the country in deposits that were clearly of Anglo-Saxon date, or at least derived from rubble resulting from the demolition of a pre-Conquest, that is pre-1066, building. What were they?

No complete tiles or fragments were found in their original position in the excavations of Old Minster in 1962–9, but nearly 500 fragments were recovered. The position of each was recorded and when these were plotted, and the layers in which the fragments were found had been tabulated, it became clear that they came from two distinct areas. One was around the original altar of the first church built in the mid seventh century. The other was in the westwork dedicated in 980. Fragments from the latter area seemed themselves to be reused, but the ones found in the area of the original high altar were from rubble used to raise the floor of the new east end dedicated in 992–4. Since pottery was not glazed in England before the mid tenth century, the tiles were probably from some redecoration around the original high altar in the 960s or before the rebuilding of the area of the altar in 992–4.

In fact, they can probably be dated precisely: King Eadred of Wessex (946–55) was buried in Old Minster and remembered as 'a particular friend and champion' who had intended, if he had lived, 'to decorate the eastern porticus of the church with golden tiles'. This cannot refer to roof tiles, which are unknown at this period, and can only refer to these polychrome-glazed relief-decorated floor tiles, whose dominant colour is a bright yellow glaze, and whose fragments were found in such numbers in the east end of the earlier church before its rebuilding and dedication in 992–4.

The tiles have at least ten different patterns. Each tile forms part of a much larger pattern which can only be understood when they are grouped in sets of sixteen. These reconstructed blocks, the patterns of which have no clear relationship one to another, can be grouped together to give some indication of how the area around the high altar might have looked (as shown in this reconstructed plan), in the years before the area was entirely remodelled (992–4).

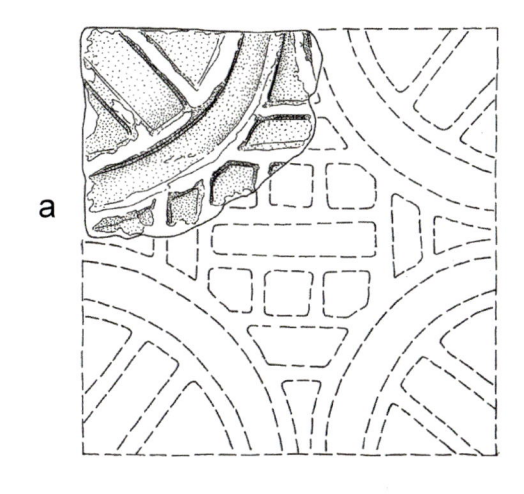

(a) a broken tile, (b) the pattern created by sixteen tiles of that same pattern, (c) a possible reconstruction of the tiled floor around the altar of Old Minster in the years between 955 and c.992–4, and how this fits into the plan of the minster before the rebuilding of this part of the church in the late 10th century.

It was probably by this date that some of the tiles had been salvaged and reused to decorate the floor of one or more of the chapels in the westwork where many more fragments were found. Having once decorated the area around the high altar they would perhaps have been prized for the memory and sanctity of their former use.

Relief decorated polychrome-glazed tiles of this kind are also known from other great monasteries, such as St Albans, Peterborough, Bury St Edmunds, and Westminster, renewed by the Benedictine reforms of the later tenth century following the example initiated by Æthelwold at Winchester in 964.

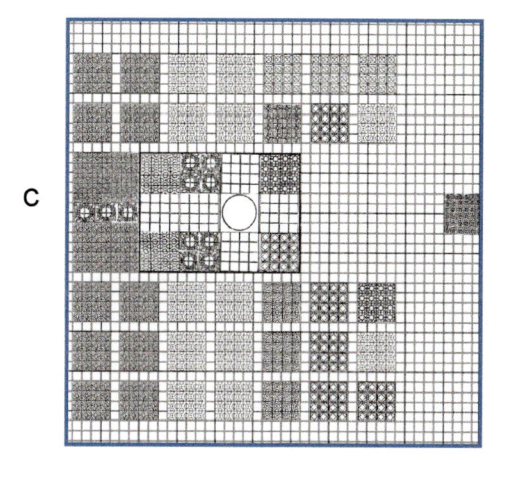

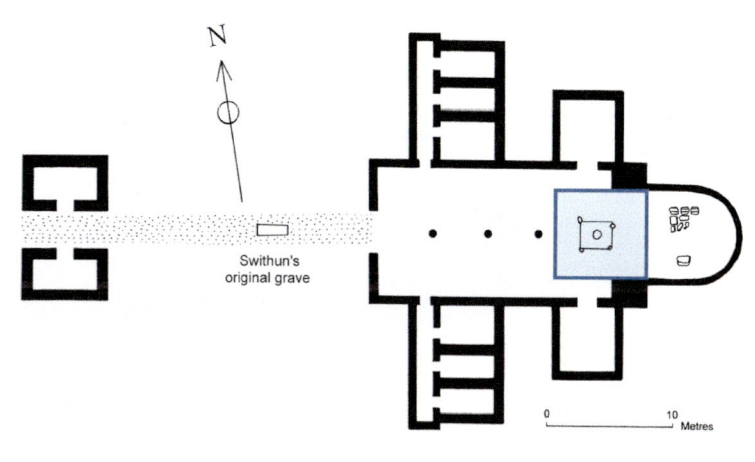

Archaeological excavations and finds

Small finds

Apart from fragments of the Old Minster itself, many objects were found during the excavation of the site of Old Minster, ranging in date from the fifth century AD to the end of the Middle Ages.

Some of these objects were symbols of the role of the deceased, notably nineteen pewter chalices, seven accompanied by a paten (a flat dish to hold the consecrated bread), which show that the burial was that of a priest. They were found only in medieval graves in the cemetery overlying the site of the demolished Old Minster. One of the priests held in his hands a mason's trowel, suggesting perhaps that he had played a role in works of building or repair, perhaps to his church. Other objects on these pages, some very fine, clearly came from the clothing in which the deceased had been buried.

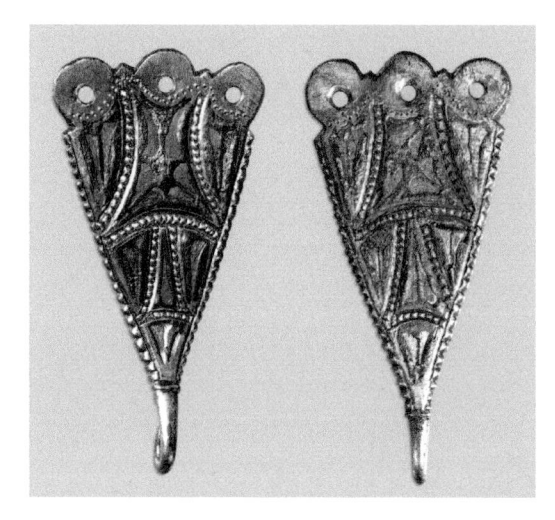

This pair of hooked silver tags, probably used for garters, was found lying at the knees of a youth of about 21–25 buried in Grave 67 inside the nave of Old Minster in the mid to late 9th century. The burial probably belonged to a member of the royal family (see p. 23). The pattern on the tags is filled with niello, a black metallic alloy (image one and a half life-size)

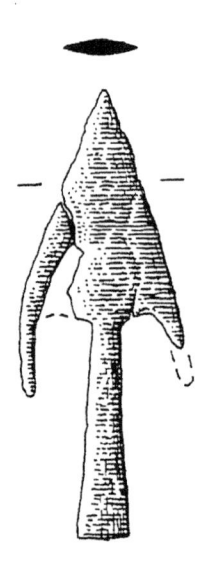

This barbed iron arrowhead was found embedded in the spine of a young adult male buried in a stone coffin set tight up against the outside of the east apse of Old Minster in Grave 124, some time in the 1050s or 1060s. Richard, second son of William the Conqueror, was killed while hunting in the New Forest about 1075, as was his younger brother William Rufus in 1100, but their remains are in the present cathedral. This burial in a stone coffin, an indication of the highest social rank, must be that of a young noble who died in yet another hunting accident. Drawing by WRU artist (image life-size)

This bowl of a liturgical spoon discovered in the rubble from the demolished east end of Old Minster is one of the finest objects found in the excavation. Carved from elephant ivory of outstanding quality, the bowl emerges from the jaws of a magnificent biting monster whose elongated body would have provided the handle. The style of carving is similar to that of a number of manuscripts written in southern England around the year 1000 (seen also in the strap-end opposite). (image one and half life-size)

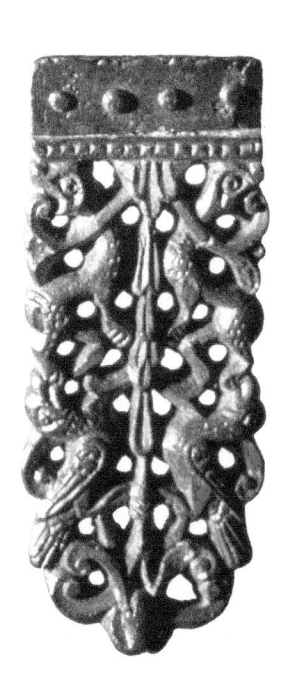

This magnificent cast bronze openwork strap-end in the 'Winchester Style' is one of the finest known from Anglo-Saxon England. It was found in Grave 321, the burial of a man who died sometime in the middle of the 10th century. Since no buckle was found, the belt was perhaps knotted with the strap-end hanging loose to display its pattern of birds and animals set among the leaves of an acanthus. (original size H: 67 mm)

This superb cast bronze plaque decorated with acanthus leaves held in a strictly controlled pattern of continuous squares was found in a late 11th-century context in the cloister of New Minster. Possibly from a wooden box or even a book cover, it has been described as 'one of the most problematical objects' found in the excavations of 1961–71. Drawing by David Hyde. (image life-size)

*(above) This fragment is from a clay mould for casting by the 'lost-wax' method a bell for the tower of Old Minster. Drawing by WRU artist. (original size: 280 x 150 mm)
In 1964 the remains of a 'bell-pit' (right) were found dug into the original floor of the nave, later covered by the floor of the new east end dedicated in 992–4 in the time of Bishop Ælfheah. The pit contained fragments of the outer or 'cope' mould from the last firing. This fragment carries the impression of letters inscribed on the wax model which would have melted away as the hot metal was poured into the mould. The letters when reversed read ISC. If the inscription was in Latin and named the person by whose order the bell was cast, the word might be EPISCOPVS, 'bishop', in which case the inscription might have read:
ÆLFEGVS EP**ISC**OPVS ME FECIT
—'Bishop Ælfheah made me'.*

Understanding the evidence

With the excavation in progress over successive summer seasons, it was often difficult, indeed impossible, to know the full significance of what was being uncovered. Final understanding had to wait not only until the end of work on site in 1970, eight years after the remarkable evidence of the 1962 trench first led to the identification of the site of Old Minster, but also until the 'post-excavation' analysis of the records and finds was complete many years later. This delay, and the impossibility of reviewing all the evidence as it was uncovered at any one moment, placed particular emphasis on the accuracy and detail of the drawn and written record of the excavation.

An indication of the eventual complexity and detail of the elements recorded during the excavation of Old Minster appears in the 71 site note-books, 45 level books, 1,986 metres of section drawings, and 10,250 square metres of plans. Every square metre was planned on average more than six times as successively earlier surfaces were uncovered.

The drawing of a vertical section through the superimposed layers of the site shown on pp. 14–15 gives an idea of the kind of record which had to be made of the layers, which had themselves been cut through and destroyed during the excavation. The making of such detailed records is the primary duty of all archaeologists.

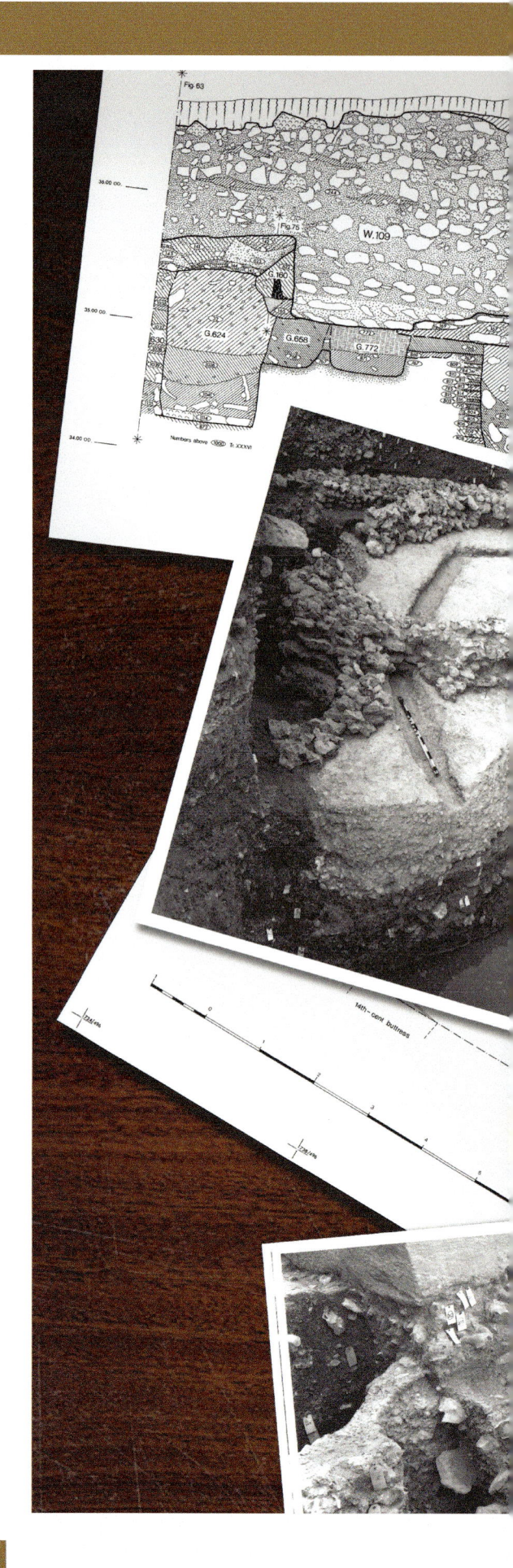

10th- cent. chalk foundation

Understanding the evidence

(left) No photograph better catches the transition between the Anglo-Saxon Old Minster and the Norman cathedral than this view taken looking west from the roof of the Norman north transept of the cathedral. The plan of Old Minster in its final form is marked out in modern brick in the grass alongside the present nave which preserves the line and much of the fabric of its Norman predecessor. The fact that the Anglo-Saxon and Norman alignments converge, suggests that both churches probably point to some lost feature further west in the precinct of the now wholly vanished royal palace of the Anglo-Saxon and Norman kings.
©John Crook

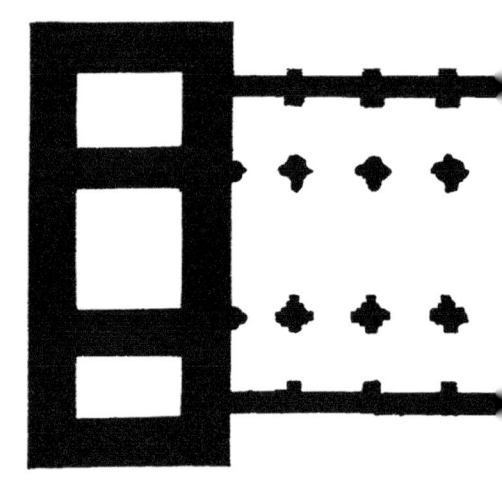

Plans, sections, and written records

A vast number of records had to be made to describe and record for posterity the evidence we were destroying in the very process of excavation (see pp. 32–3), but we had an additional problem: when the excavations began on the Cathedral Car Park in 1961, imperial measurements in feet and inches were universal. Notes, mainly consisting of layer descriptions, were written in 'Science Books' with lined pages facing graph paper printed in inches and tenths(!) or twelfths; plans were drawn by triangulation from fixed pegs, as recommended in Sir Mortimer Wheeler's *Archaeology from the Earth* (1954), and recorded on non-standard sheets of graph paper; vertical sections were drawn, usually at a scale of 1 inch or ½ inch to the foot (1:12 or 1:24), also on non-standard sheets of graph paper; Ordnance Datum (OD) heights were rarely recorded. Colour was almost never used on plans or sections (and unfortunately still is not used much today).

All this changed over the winter of 1964–5 with the recognition of the need for greater precision and standardisation of the records and record keeping. The metric system was introduced for the 1965 season on all excavations then in progress throughout the city under the aegis of the Winchester Excavations Committee. 'Cartesian' co-ordinate grids were set up for the planning of each site and the systematic use of the surveyor's level was introduced for

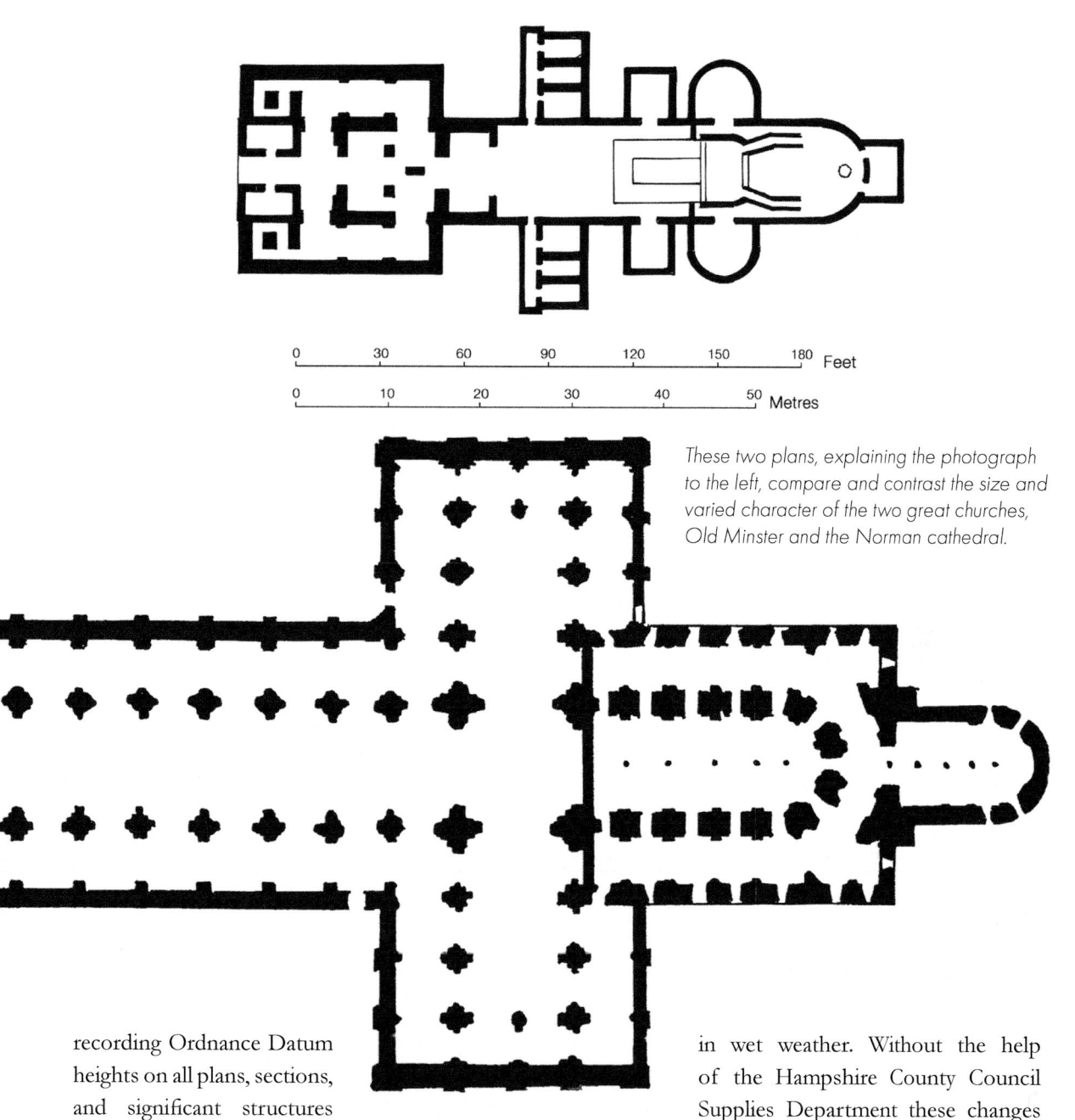

These two plans, explaining the photograph to the left, compare and contrast the size and varied character of the two great churches, Old Minster and the Norman cathedral.

recording Ordnance Datum heights on all plans, sections, and significant structures and deposits. At the peak of Mr Harold Wilson's 'white heat of the technological revolution', we found it very difficult to obtain the necessary tapes, surveying staffs, and ranging rods, and had to have the metal grids we needed for planning within the co-ordinate system manufactured to our own specification. At the same time standard sheets of weather-proof plastic film, pre-printed with a metric grid at 1 mm, 5 mm, and 10 mm intervals, and an imposed grid at 50 mm, were introduced in place of the use of non-standard sheets of graph paper, which were subject to damage and distortion in wet weather. Without the help of the Hampshire County Council Supplies Department these changes would perhaps have been impossible. But the primary influence on the abandonment of the older 'traditional' and out-dated archaeological practices was undoubtedly the arrival as a volunteer on the excavation of Old Minster in the summer of 1964 of Birthe Kjølbye, then studying for a magister degree in archaeology at the University of Aarhus in Denmark. Despite some initial resistance, the practices and systems adopted at Winchester in the winter of 1964–5 were rapidly to become standard throughout British archaeology, and many remain so today.

Understanding the evidence

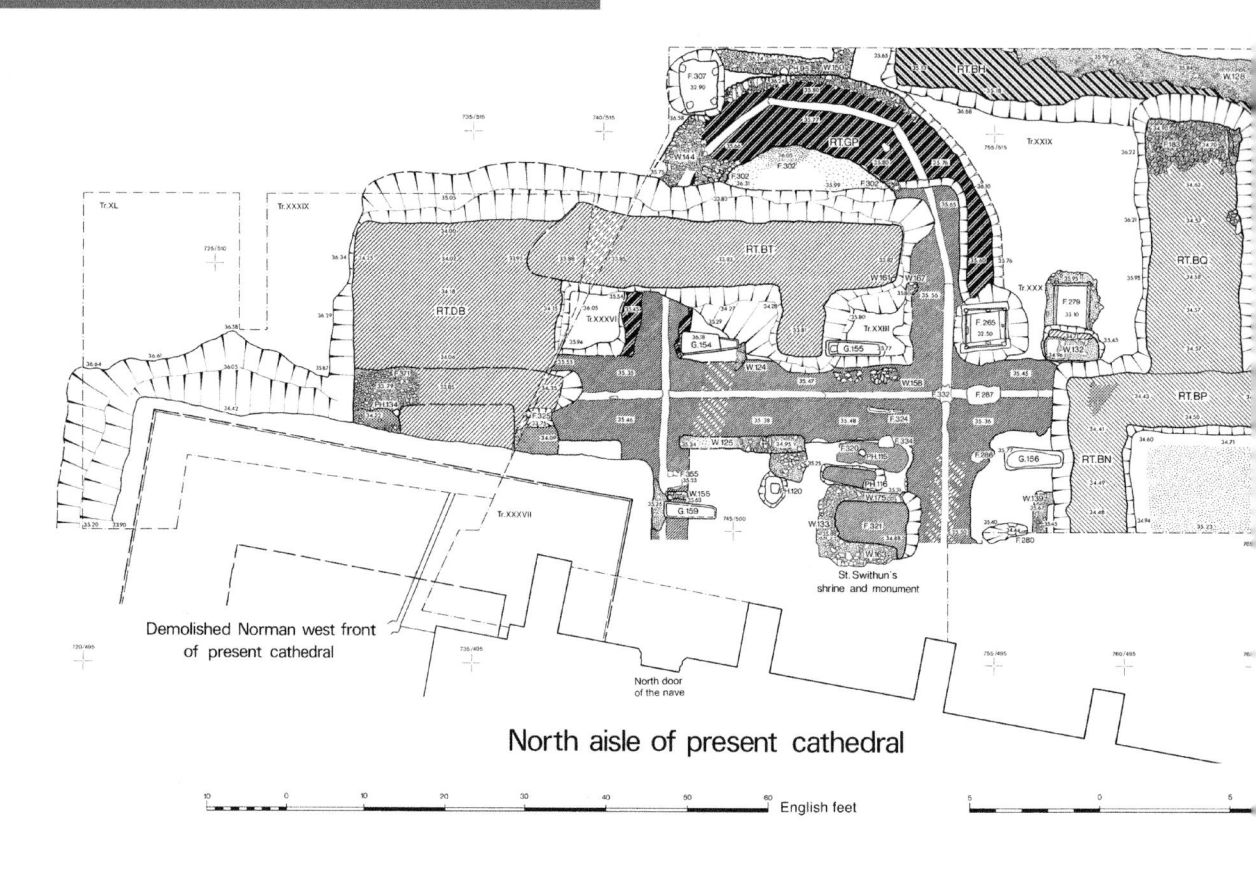

(above) This plan shows all the surviving remains of Old Minster as they were found by excavation. It includes foundations where these survived. Where the foundations did not survive, the plan shows the outlines of the bottom of the robber-trenches. These outlines are taken to represent the closest available approximation to the outline of the foundations which had been removed.

Robber-trenches

Once the evidence of archaeology had begun to come into play the sites of the Old and New Minsters were rapidly identified, but it also revealed a fundamental problem. The walls of Old Minster were no longer there and were represented only by the trenches filled in with the rubble left behind by the demolition gangs. Not content with removing the entire standing structure to recover material for use in building the nave of the Norman cathedral, the demolition gangs had dug out virtually every piece of reusable stone they could find in the foundations, leaving behind trenches filled only with useless fragments of stone, mortar, and plaster. Archaeologists call these 'robber-trenches'. They provide almost the only evidence for the plan of a building so thoroughly demolished as Old Minster had been.

Stone-robbers do no more work than is absolutely necessary. Conditions were often, perhaps usually chaotic, producing piles of rubble in all directions. Sometimes it was simply too much effort for the demolition gang to move rubble in order to extract reusable stones which had been missed and had become covered up. Thus, fragments of earlier walls still survived, haphazard and unexpected.

It also soon became clear that the width of a robber-trench provided a reasonably accurate idea of the width and line of the wall being robbed, or often more particularly of its foundations. The depth of the robber-trench

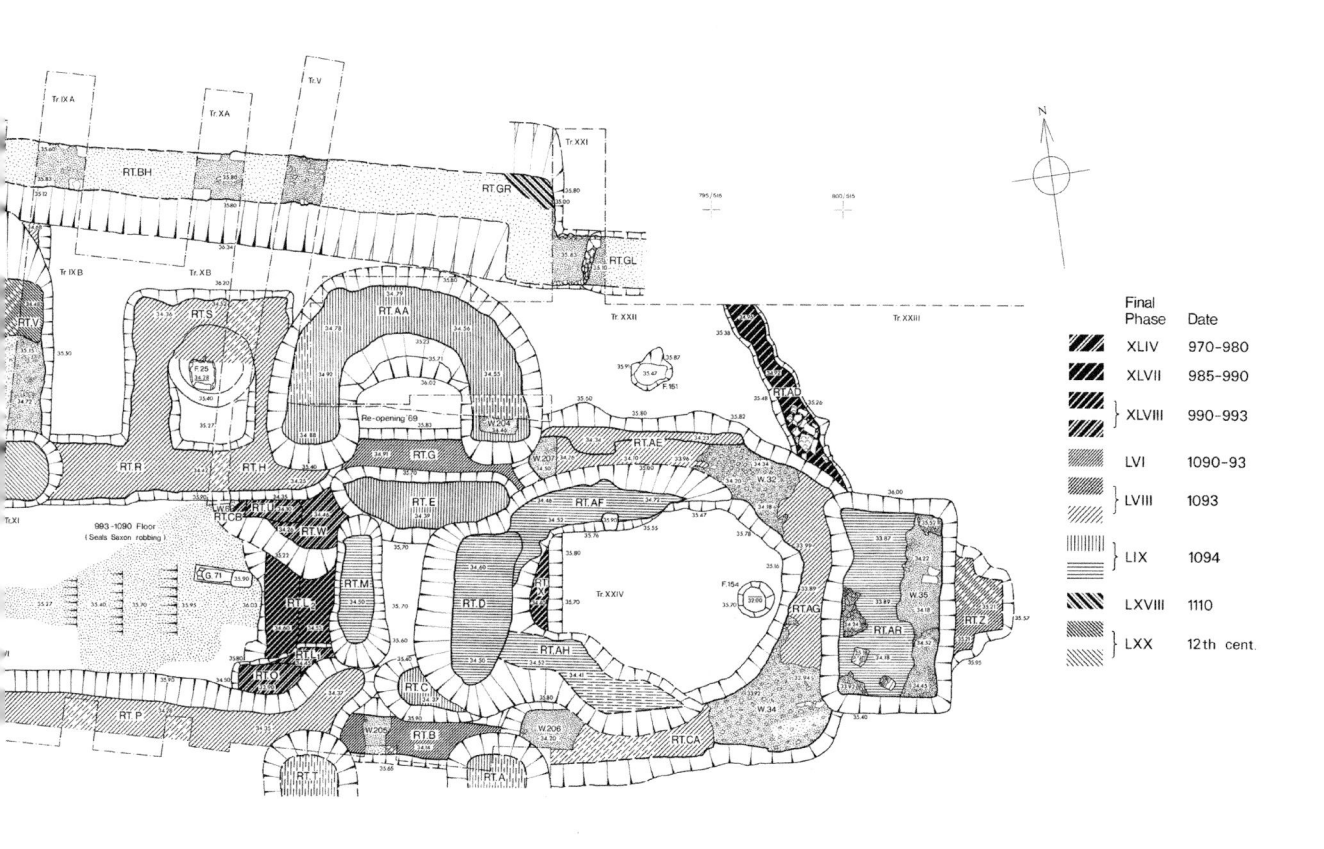

Final Phase	Date
XLIV	970–980
XLVII	985–990
XLVIII	990–993
LVI	1090–93
LVIII	1093
LIX	1094
LXVIII	1110
LXX	12th cent.

(right) This remarkable drawing by Simon Hayfield shows the whole of the robbed site of Old Minster as it might have looked after the Norman builders of the new cathedral had taken away all the stone they could reuse. The site never appeared like this of course: the work proceeded piecemeal, and the robbed-out areas were covered with mounds of useless debris as the work of robbing went on. Nevertheless, the drawing gives a vivid idea of the extent to which almost every part of the building below ground, as well as all the standing walls and roofs, had been removed.

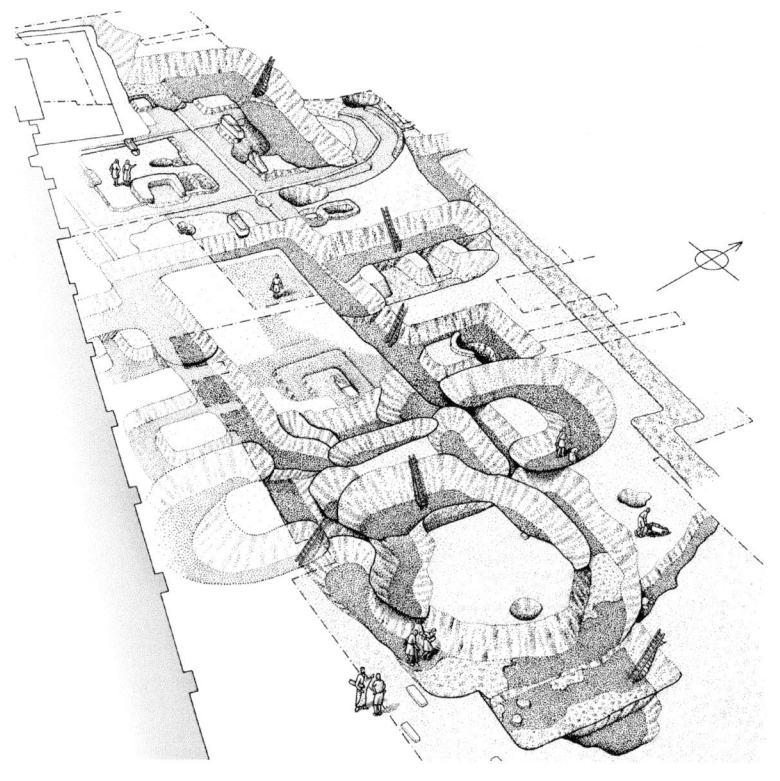

was equally important. If the bottom stepped up or down, it was usually because the original depth of the wall or foundation had changed. This provided a vital clue to the structural sequence of the building, indicating perhaps the point at which walls of two different types, founded at different depths, had butted up against each other, either because the load to be carried had changed, or because walls on foundations of two different building periods had been removed.

Understanding the evidence

Interpreting the plans

The east end of the original seventh-century church provides a clear example of how a vanished superstructure can be reconstructed when only the foundations survive.

The walls of the earliest Old Minster were built on broad foundations of broken and reused Roman tiles separated by courses of Roman rubble. The foundation trenches were dug to an even depth throughout and ran at an angle across a Roman street, the presence of which was ignored. Of the footing walls laid on the level surface provided by these foundations, only four blocks of reused green sandstone survived in position; the remainder, and all the walls standing on the footings, had been removed by the Norman stone-robbing.

The plan preserved by the foundations, together with indications left by later additions and in the pattern of the robbing, allowed the plan of the first church to be recovered.

The church was built on a cross-plan comprising a nave – a double square, 22 metres long and 11 metres wide externally – with a narrower eastern chamber or porticus and smaller rooms to north and south. Cross-plans of this type dating from the sixth century onwards are characteristic of northern Italy and adjacent areas. The plan, the sophistication of the ratios behind it, and the surveying skills, although simple, required to lay the plan out on the ground, and an understanding of the technology needed to support heavy stone buildings, suggest that the first church at Winchester was built while Birinus or members of his Italian mission were still alive to influence its design and construction.

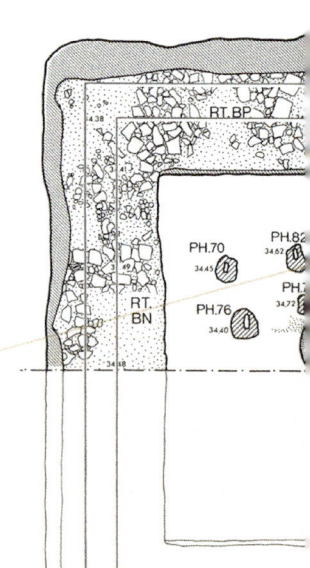

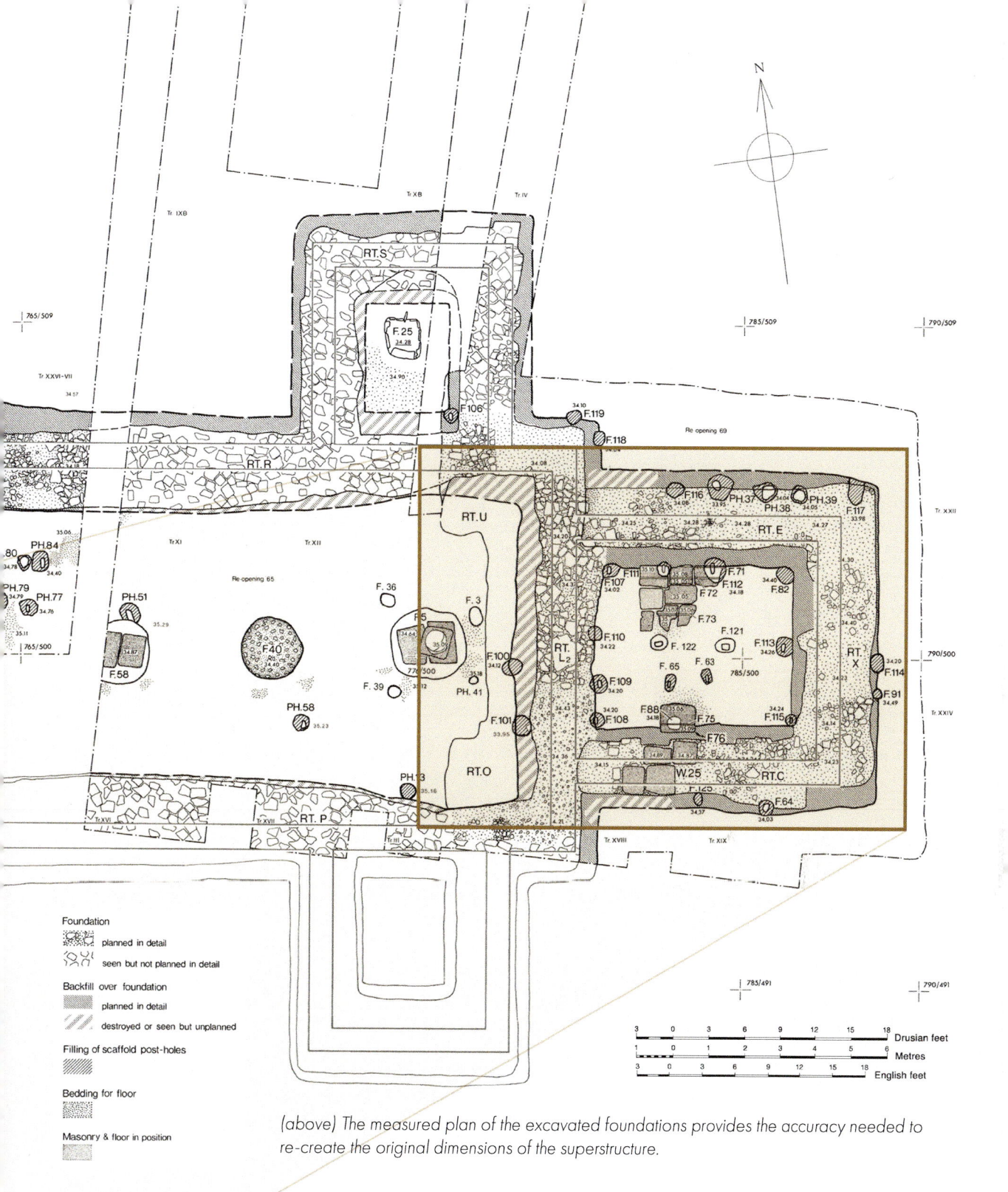

(above) The measured plan of the excavated foundations provides the accuracy needed to re-create the original dimensions of the superstructure.

(left) This photograph of the excavated foundations show the character and nature of the surviving evidence. The rectangle of pink rubble which dominates this photograph is formed of broken Roman tiles and other rubble used to lay the foundations of the rectangular east arm or 'porticus' of the first church built about 650.

The stone foundation for the altar of the 7th-century church (see illustration on p. 16 above) can be seen to the left at the edge of the excavation. Four surviving blocks of the footing for the south wall of the porticus stand on the pink rubble of the foundation immediately to the left of the scale. Nine or so slabs of light coloured oolite stone forming the original floor of the porticus lie in position in the central square. The area shown corresponds to the area tinted brown on the adjacent drawing which shows the east arm in the context of the excavation of the whole of the first church.

Understanding the evidence

The first church and its extensions

The plan of Old Minster as first built and its subsequent enlargements (pp. 42–3) are too complicated to have been created without some guiding rules. The unit of measurement appears to have been the 'Long Roman foot' (equivalent to 0.333 metre) which was used in setting out both the original seventh-century building and its later extensions. The process of laying out the building was simple and also remained unchanged over three and a half centuries (c.650 to 992–4). Both are demonstrated here by the example of the eastern extension of the church completed and dedicated by 992–4.

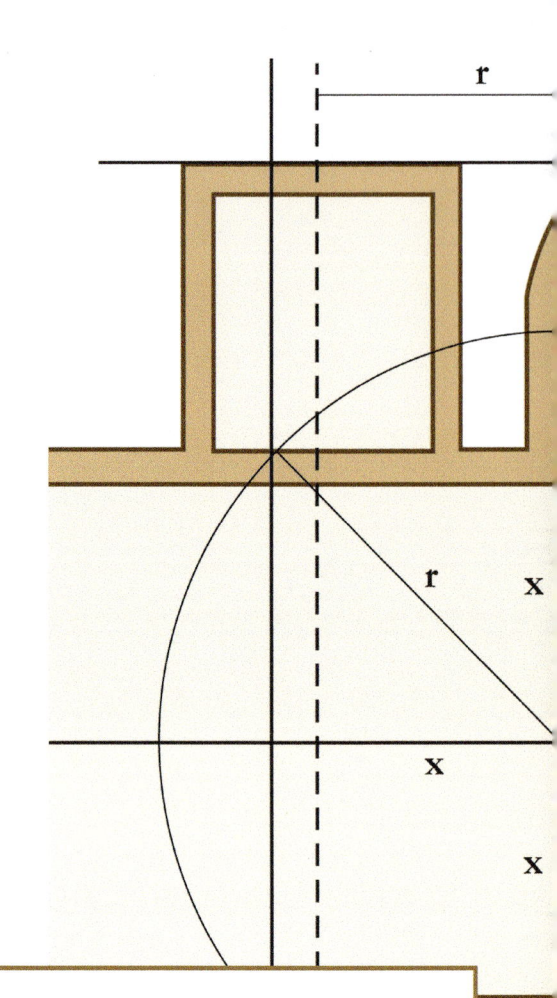

Marking out the ground-plan of the east end

As with all previous stages of Old Minster from the seventh century onwards, the plan of the east end added to Old Minster between 980 and 992–4 was actually based on a very simple geometry which could easily be laid out on the ground by two men with pegs and measuring ropes or rods. The foundation trenches would then be dug, and the foundations laid. The precise plan of the walls would then be marked on the upper surface of the foundations for the masons to follow when building the walls.

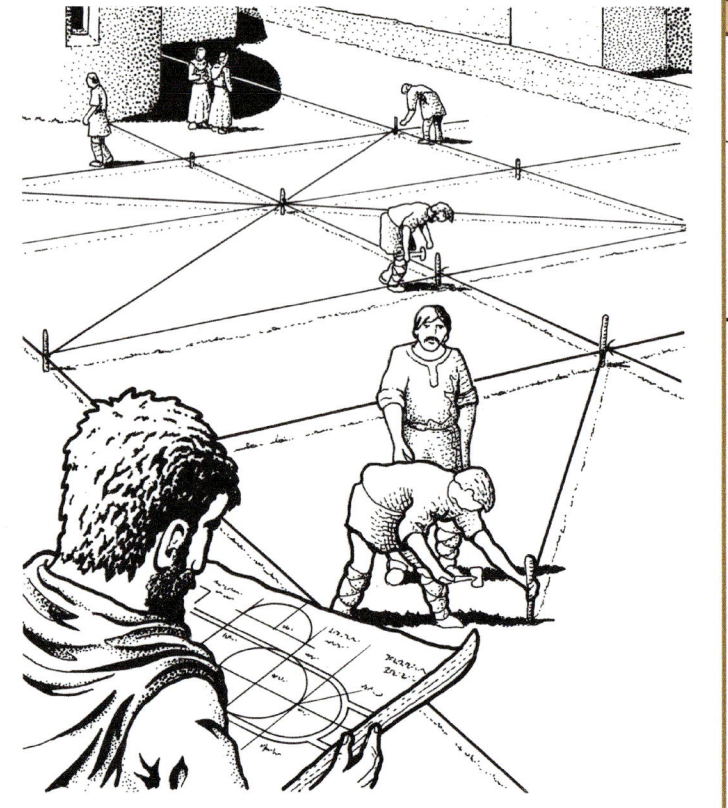

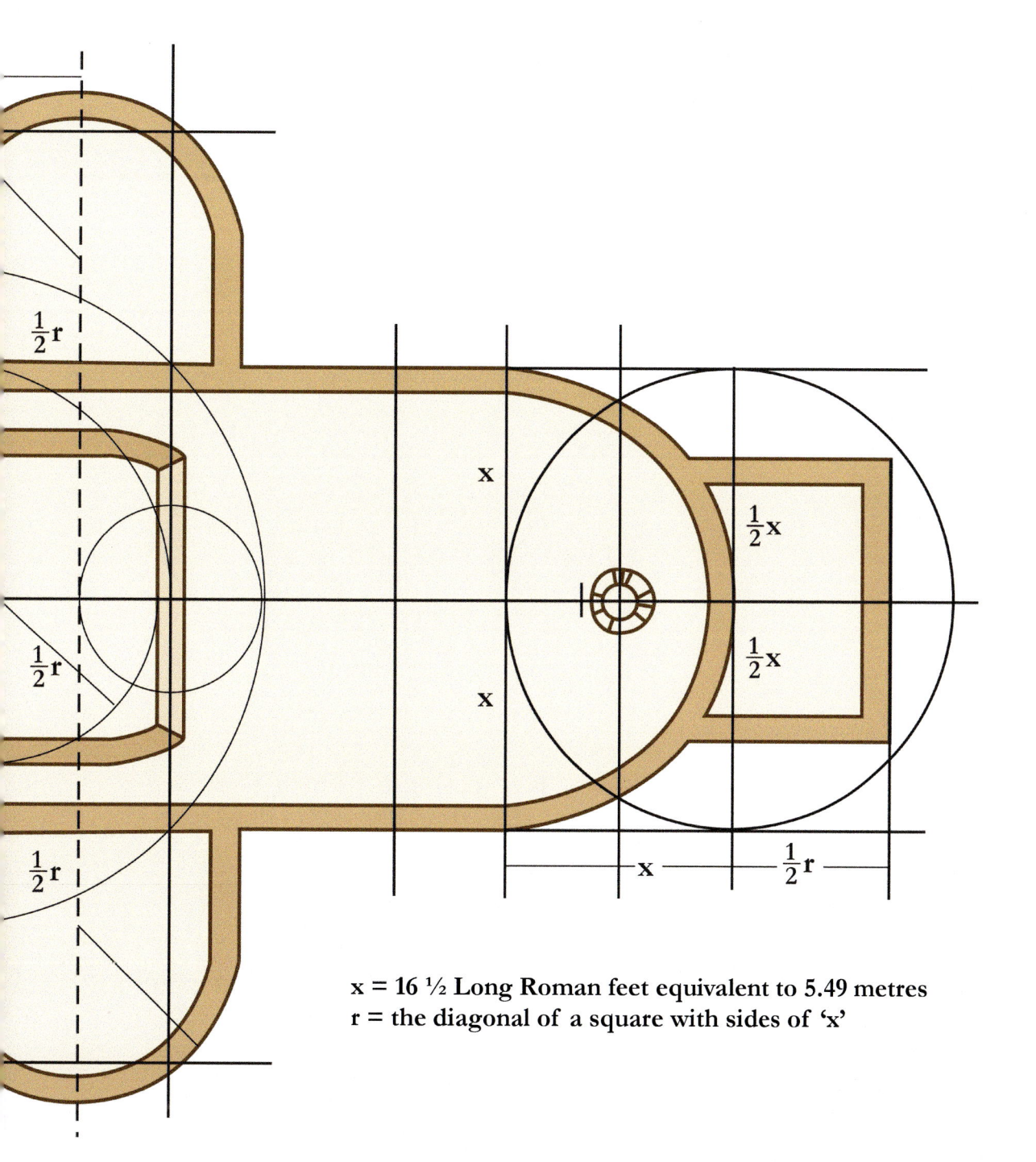

x = 16 ½ Long Roman feet equivalent to 5.49 metres
r = the diagonal of a square with sides of 'x'

The geometry of the extended east end of Old Minster

As first built in the mid seventh century, Old Minster was constructed on a simple geometric plan (p. 42, *c*.650) using the 'Long Roman' foot of 0.333 metre and a module of 16½ feet (5.49 metres, marked as 'x' on the plan above), equivalent to the Anglo-Saxon rod as used in Wessex. Such a plan could have been laid out on the ground with a few pegs and a measuring rope. This simplicity appears again, as seen below, in the great rebuilding of the later tenth century (p. 43, 992–4). Knowledge of the unit used and the principles involved were presumably preserved in the memory of the community in texts and drawings kept among its records. This extract (above) from Winchester Studies, 4.i (forthcoming), gives some idea of both the complexity of the objective and the simplicity of the underlying geometry.

Understanding the evidence

*c.*650

*c.*725–50

*c.*750–70

▨ *c.*905
▧ *c.*930

Swithun's original grave

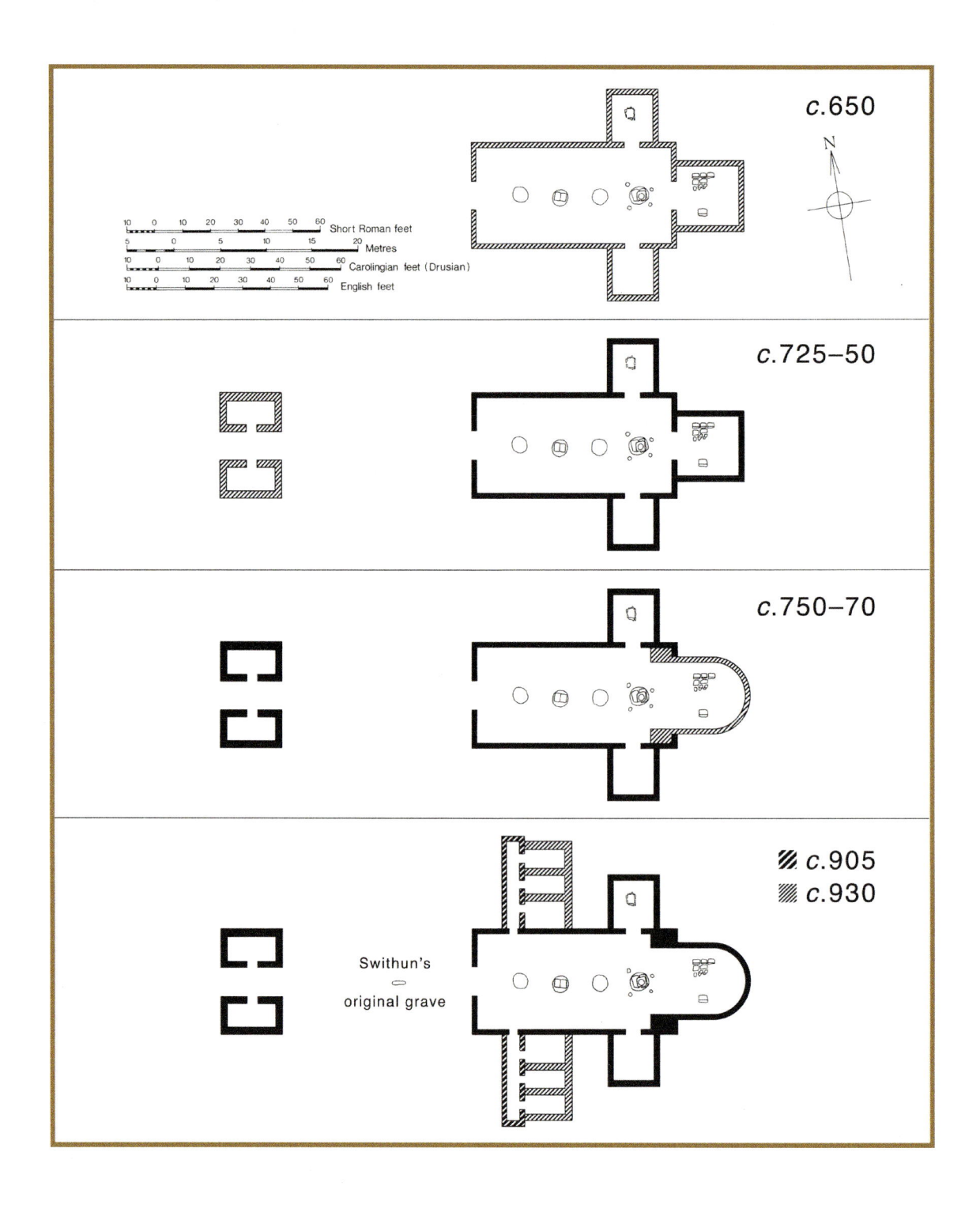

Working from the robber-trenches (pp. 36–7), using hints provided by scraps of foundations and floors, and observing how walls of different periods had butted one against another, accurate plans could be constructed of Old Minster at every stage in its development. This revealed seven distinct periods in its growth. The original church was built about 650 as a cross. A century later a gatehouse was added to the west, and a little later the original east end was given an apse. Bishop Swithun was buried in 863 in the open space between the gatehouse and the west door of the minster. Shortly after New Minster had been built to the north, a western façade was

971–5

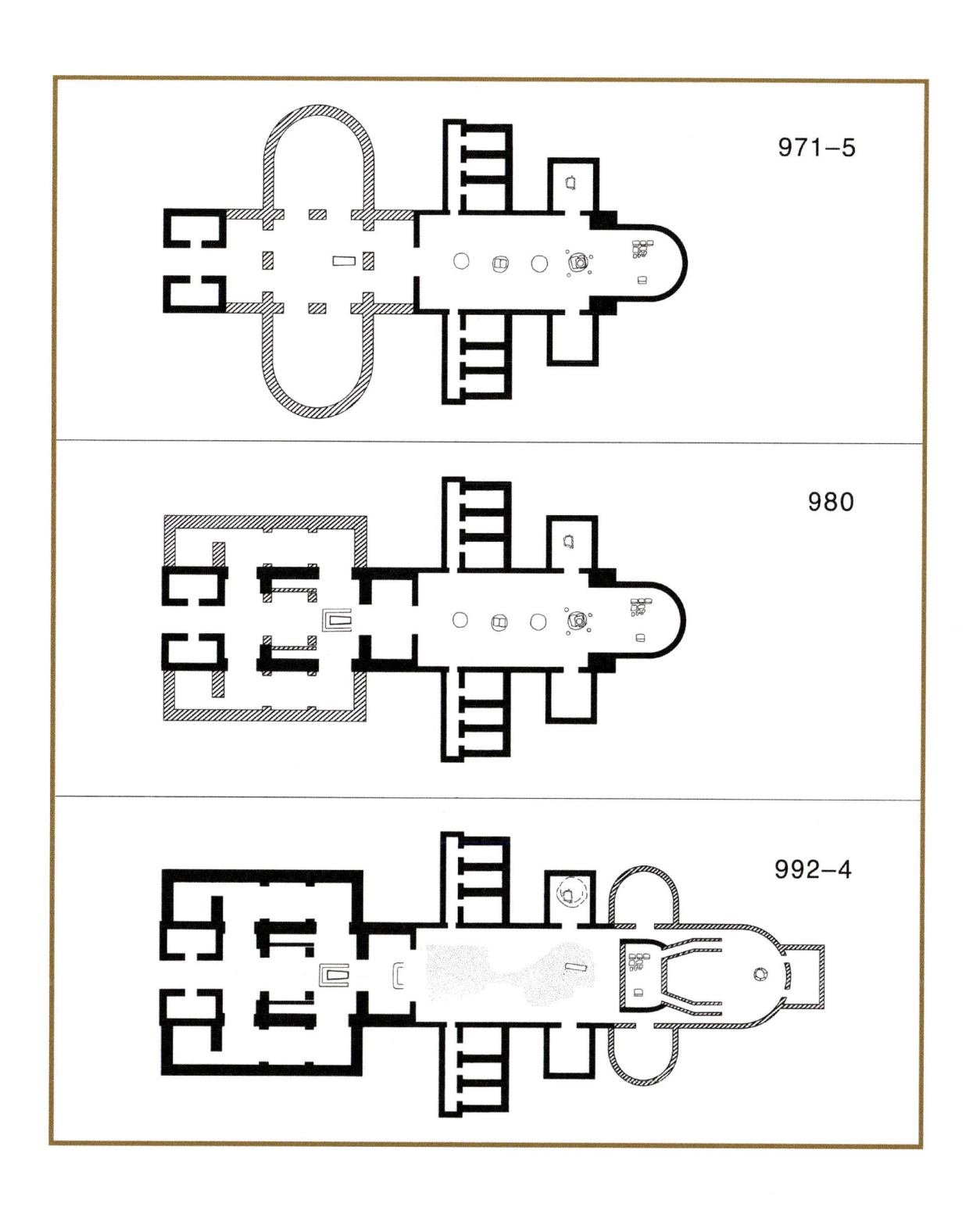

980

992–4

added c.905 to give the impression that Old Minster, when approached from the west, was even larger than New Minster. A few years later six chapels were built behind the façade. In 971 St Swithun's body was moved into the church. Immediately a vast building with two apses was constructed around the site of the saint's original grave. This building was too daring. Its foundations failed and it was rebuilt as a huge square tower dedicated in 980. In the years up to 992–4 the east end was also rebuilt with an eastern and two lateral apses, focused on the high altar where St Swithun's body now lay in a jewel-encrusted golden shrine.

Evolution of Old Minster

The first church, c.650

This church was probably the first stone building to have been constructed in the area since the Roman period, 250 years before. The fact that the Anglo-Saxon Chronicle says that King Cenwalh *het atimbran*, literally 'had timbered', in the sense 'had built', the church at Winchester, shows how unusual building in stone was even much later when the Chronicle entry was written.

The original stone floor of the church had been removed, except in the eastern annexe, but some features remained (pp. 38–9). The massive stone base of the altar, found in the 1963 excavation, lay at the east end of the nave, immediately in front of the opening to the eastern annexe. Down the centre-line of the nave there were three further massive foundations, mostly robbed, of unknown function, possibly intended to support stone crosses with additional altars. The northern annexe contained a well, probably indicating the position of the baptistery.

Although the walls of the first church had not survived, the depth and strength of the foundations, and the provision of massive footings built of reused stones of Roman origin, show that this was a masonry building. Nothing is known of the detail of its doors and windows. The roof was probably thatched or shingled, but it is not impossible that it was leaded, for reusable lead might have been obtainable, like stone and tile, from the ruins of Roman buildings, not least from the vast forum of Roman *Venta* which had stood immediately to the north of the site chosen for the church.

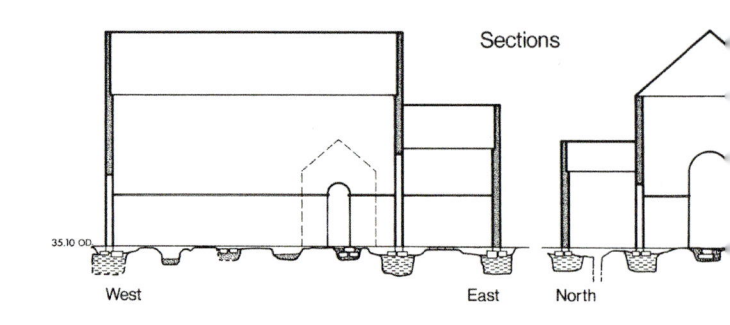

Elevations

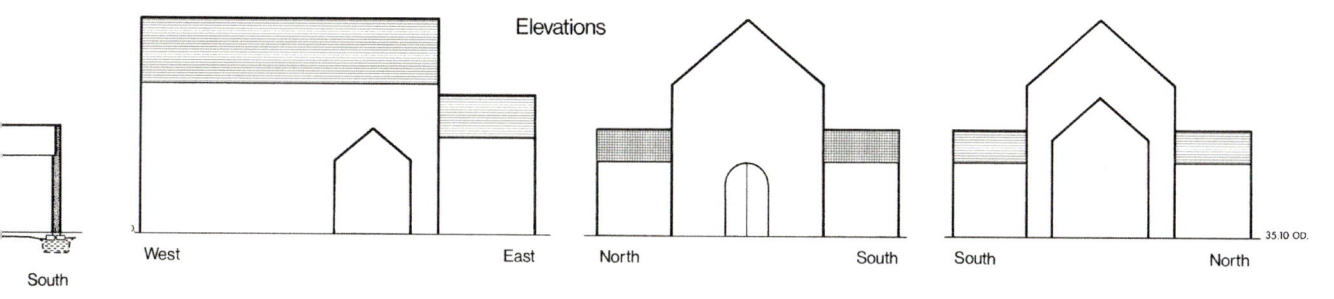

South West East North South South North

c.650 Reconstructions of the sections and elevations of the first church.

As first built, the church had a large nave with a narrower east end ('chancel') and smaller chapels to north and south. Only the foundations survived, but the painting gives an idea of what Old Minster may have looked like when first built about 650.

45

Evolution of Old Minster

c.725–50. About the middle of the 8th century a substantial gatehouse dedicated to St Martin was built to the west of Old Minster, at the entrance to its precinct and cemetery.

Burials, an apse, and the building of St Martin's Tower, seventh to ninth centuries

There were fifteen bishops of Winchester from Wine (660–?663) to Helmstan (?838–?852). We know little about most of them except for their approximate dates but they provide evidence of an unbroken continuity of worship, confirmed by the eight successive 'generations' of burials which during these two centuries clustered on all sides around the church.

There is no written record of changes to the building: for that we must turn to archaeology. Around the mid eighth century a free-standing tower, of which only the north wall was found, was built 20 metres in front of the west door of the nave (p. 42). Later recorded as dedicated to St Martin, this was perhaps a gatehouse giving entry to the precinct and its surrounding graveyard. At about the same date the square eastern annexe of the first church was rebuilt as an apse.

c.905. Shortly after the building in 901–3 of New Minster (seen in outline to the left), substantial wings were added north and south of the west front of Old Minster, giving the impression that Old Minster, when seen from the front, was the larger of the two.

The building of New Minster, 901–3, and the reaction of Old Minster

In 901 King Edward the Elder of Wessex (899–924) obtained land on which to found a new minster on a site immediately north of the existing church, which henceforth was known as Old Minster. Although his father, King Alfred, had died in 899 and had been buried in Old Minster, Edward apparently decided to build a new church as a burial place for his father and mother and their descendants (see pp. 66–8).

In addition to the land north of Old Minster, a further strip (including part of Old Minster's cemetery) was acquired, so that the new church could be built within a yard of the north wall of the earlier church. The agreements are minutely detailed – with measurements – in a contemporary record, but there is no indication why so awkward an arrangement was made. Excavation showed that the nave alone of the new church was to occupy twice the area of the Old Minster church as it then stood (see p. 67).

c.930. Old Minster seen from the east, showing the apse of the rebuilt east end of c.770 and the triple chapels added c.930 to the east side of the north and south wings of c.905.

To this evident slight must be added the loss to Old Minster of the royal burial of King Alfred with the prestige it bore.

In the next few years the community of Old Minster reacted by building what seem to be wings to either side of the west front of their church (p. 42). The whole of the north wing was excavated in 1966–8. The south wing lies below the nave of the present cathedral, but it seems fair to suppose that it mirrored the north wing. If so, a visitor approaching from the west would get the impression that Old Minster was by far the larger of the two churches, 30 metres in width, compared with the width of 20 metres of the New Minster nave. These wings (if correctly seen as lying to both sides of the Old Minster nave) had deep foundations and were presumably correspondingly tall, consisting of massively thick walls which may have contained passages and staircases. A decade or so later three chapels were added to the east side of the north wing and presumably also to the unexcavated wing to the south (p. 42).

Evolution of Old Minster

Bishop Æthelwold (963–84), monastic reform, and the translation of St Swithun

Æthelwold, then abbot of Abingdon, a leading scholar and teacher and a central figure in the monastic reform of the later tenth century, was appointed bishop of Winchester late in 963. The following year he forcibly expelled the secular canons from Old Minster and replaced them with Benedictine monks from Abingdon living under a strict rule. Soon afterwards he did the same at New Minster and established nuns at Nunnaminster. The document known as *Regularis Concordia*, 'the norm for reformed Benedictine monasticism in England', issued at the council of Winchester in 973, was Æthelwold's work.

From 968 onwards a series of miracles of healing were believed to be taking place at the grave of Bishop Swithun outside the west door of Old Minster. On 15 July 971 Bishop Æthelwold supervised the opening of his predecessor's grave. The body lay in a stone sarcophagus under a stone lid in which six iron rings were set for letting it down. Swithun's remains were taken up and 'translated' to a temporary shrine inside the church (see pp. 16–19). Over the next months a magnificent jewelled golden reliquary was made at King Edgar's estate, probably that at King's Somborne to the west of Winchester, and brought in procession into the city and placed in Old Minster, perhaps on 8 October 971. The many miracles believed to have taken place at the new shrine were recorded at length in subsequent years by Winchester scholars such as Lantfred, Wulfstan the Cantor, and Ælfric.

Æthelwold now set about rebuilding Old Minster on an immense scale. He extended the existing nave across the open space between it and St Martin's Tower, enclosing the site of

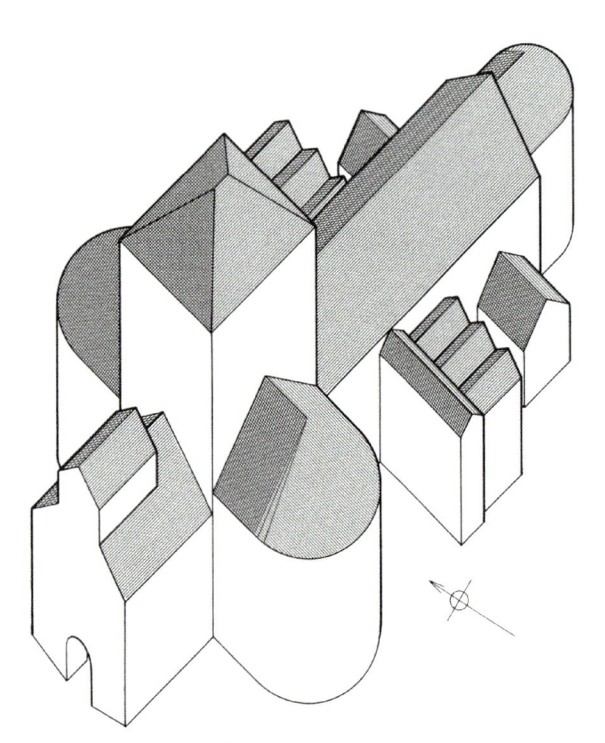

Axonometric view of Old Minster c.975 looking north-east, showing the tower over the grave of St Swithun (d. 863), flanked to north and south by apses to either side of his grave.

St Swithun's grave and building huge apses to either side. These measured overall from north to south exactly 100 Long Roman feet (each Long Roman foot measures about 13.15 of our inches, or 0.333 metre), a length precisely equal to the internal diameter of the rotunda surrounding the Tomb of Christ in Jerusalem. This is no chance: whether derived directly from Jerusalem or from the external diameter of the rotunda which Charlemagne (d. 814) erected at his palace in Aachen, such a huge, sophisticated structure surrounding the site of the saint's original grave is the most astonishing building constructed in Anglo-Saxon England up to this time – a clear sign of the honour with which Bishop Æthelwold intended to celebrate the miracle-working Swithun.

Almost at once the building failed. Erected on foundations of puddled and rammed chalk, laced with timber beams, it had been erected partly on top of, and partly off the line of, an underlying Roman street which passed at an angle below the site. The foundations broke over the softer ground lying beside the packed gravel of the Roman street. This must have caused cracks to appear in the rising wall of the northern apse (the southern apse lies in mirror image below the nave of the present cathedral and was not seen by us).

(above) Looking north across the chalk foundations of c.975 for the northern apse and the north wall of the western tower of the intended martyrium. The remains and site of the shrine around the grave of St Swithun are marked 'S'.

(below) c.975. View looking north-west along the south side of Old Minster with the western tower and apsed martyrium of St Swithun as originally intended.

Evolution of Old Minster

Rebuilding (975–80)

A new start was made. A huge square tower was erected on solid foundations of mortared flint set in deep trenches cut to an even depth. This is a 'westwork', a structure which has close surviving parallels in Germany, particularly at the Imperial abbey at Corvey on the Weser.

Corvey is hardly likely to have been the model for the Winchester westwork. It is more likely that both Winchester and Corvey were modelled on a westwork, no longer surviving and known only from engravings, which stood at the monastery of Corbie on the Somme in Picardy.

Old Minster looking north-east, showing the westwork built over the grave of St Swithun as dedicated on 20 October 980.

(right) The west front of the imperial abbey of Corvey (Rhine-Westfalen, Germany), built 873–85. (Courtesy of Westfälisches Museum für Archäologie, Münster)

Corvey in Germany was founded from Corbie (as its name implies); Bishop Æthelwold was in close contact with Corbie in France, from which he borrowed settings for the Mass.

The great structure in Winchester was dedicated on 20 October 980 in the presence of King Æthelred, nine bishops, and the leading men of

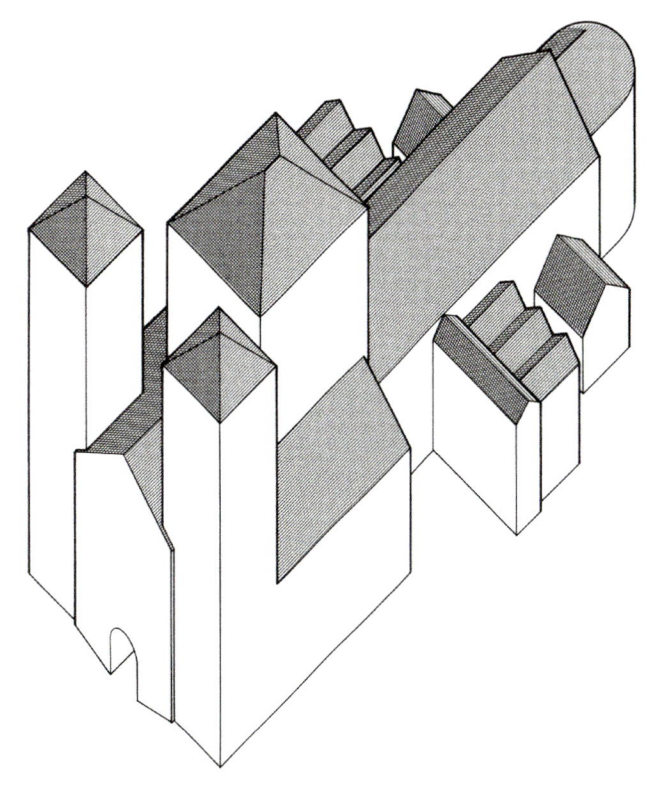

(above) Axonometric view of Old Minster 980, looking north-east, showing the westwork over the grave of St Swithun as dedicated on 20 October 980.

the kingdom, in an event lasting two days, celebrated in Latin verse by the cantor (we would say precentor) Wulfstan, the biographer of Bishop Æthelwold.

At the heart of the new westwork a tall shrine now stood on the site where St Swithun had been buried in 863. Further to the east, at the east end of the nave, the coffin in which he had originally been buried was now placed on the north side of the main altar at which he himself must so often have celebrated Mass.

The completion of the west end in 980 was only the first part of Bishop Æthelwold's rebuilding of Old Minster. He now began work on the extension and rebuilding of the east end, laying out three apses, one each to north and south, flanking the new principal altar, with a third stretching far to the east and ending in a rectangular crypt. Æthelwold died in 984 leaving the completion of the campaign of reconstruction to Ælfheah, his successor as bishop of Winchester.

Evolution of Old Minster

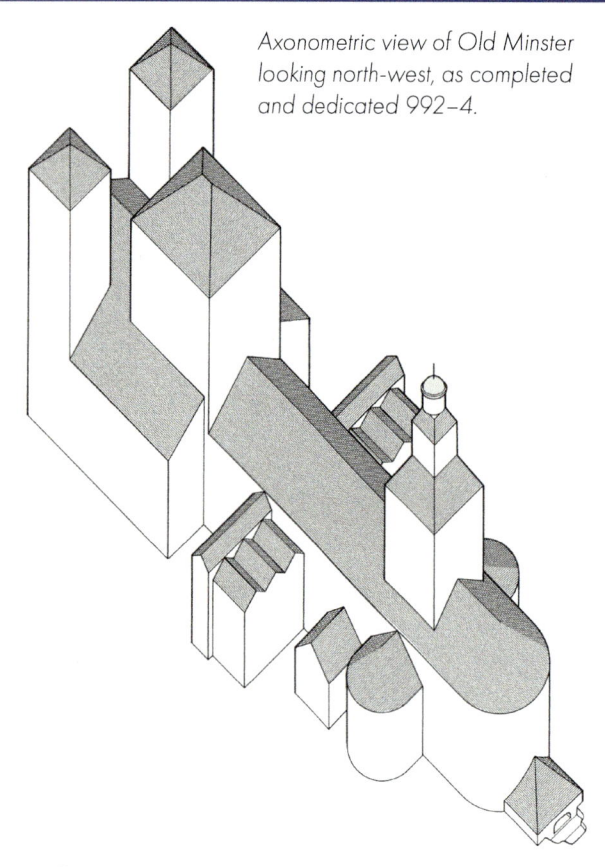

Axonometric view of Old Minster looking north-west, as completed and dedicated 992–4.

Completion 992–4

The new east end completed in 992–4 and dedicated by Bishop Ælfheah, was even more remarkable than the work of the west end begun twenty years before. Although completely demolished in 1093–4, there is now for the first time not only the evidence of archaeology, but a written description in Latin verse of some 150 lines and a contemporary illustration. The description is set out in five sections dealing with the eastern porticus, the crypts, the organs, the tower, and the dedication.

The principal altar of the new east end was now raised over a crypt formed in what had been the east end of the original church of about 650. The raised altar was approached from the west by a wide flight of broad steps. On the north side of the steps the original stone coffin of St Swithun had now been raised slightly to conform to the new level of the floor.

(right) Old Minster as completed 992–4, looking north-west.

High above the nave altar, the contemporary illustration (see p. 55) shows a timber tower of three stages crowned by a weather vane in the form of a golden cockerel. In the lowest stage of the tower, the minster's peal of five bells of different sizes were hung at two levels. The drawing also shows that the highest stage of the tower, directly below the weather cock, was round rather than square.

This arrangement is seen also on an architectural drawing of *c.*1000 from the abbey at Fleury at

Saint-Benoît-sur-Loire (with which Old Minster was in contact), where the round element is labelled *rotundus* and flanked by sleeping soldiers with their shields. This suggests that the highest level of the Old Minster tower was a representation of the Tomb of Christ in Jerusalem, often shown on ninth- and tenth century ivories as a round structure held aloft by a staged tower. If so, the place of Christ's resurrection was shown on the tower of Old Minster directly above the altar at which the body and blood of Christ were daily manifest in the Eucharist.

Ælfheah became archbishop of Canterbury in 1006 but was murdered by the Danes in 1012 in the new wave of Viking attacks which had begun in 1006. King Æthelred Unræd (not the 'unready' but the 'ill-advised') died in April 1016 and was succeeded by his third son Edmund, 'called Ironside because of his valour'. Edmund was defeated by the Danish Cnut at the battle of 'Assandun' in October and died in late November. Cnut was now recognised as king of all England and in 1017 he married Emma of Normandy, widow of King Æthelred.

Evolution of Old Minster

With the extension of the east end completed in 992–4 Old Minster had reached its final form (see also pp. 58–9). The west end was marked by twin towers and by a massive central tower rising over the site of the original grave of St Swithun. The east end and the high altar, with the shrine containing the bones of St Swithun, was flanked by apses to north, south, and east with, we believe, a staged tower containing a peal of bells and crowned by a golden weathercock (see also pp. 52–3).

(below) Old Minster as completed 992–4 from the south-west with New Minster in the background.

(right) The three-storey tower over the high altar of Old Minster, looking south, drawn about 994 by an artist illuminating the 'Benedictional of St Æthelwold'. The bells are pulled by a rope which passes down through a hole in the roof. The dome over the top storey rises from a curved base showing that the top storey itself is round. The high rod of the weather vane carries a golden weather-cock. Enlarged detail of f. 118v of The Benedictional of St Æthelwold, Add. MS. 49598. (© The British Library Board)

(above) Old Minster (to the south, left) and New Minster, side by side ('so close that a man could scarcely walk between them') looking west from St Giles's Hill, as they may have looked for the last Anglo-Saxon century (from the 990s until Old Minster was demolished in 1093–4).

Evolution of Old Minster

It is much more difficult to give an idea of the interior of the east end, the liturgical heart of the minster. The architecture is simple and the structure of the roof was probably visible, but we have no idea how the walls were treated. Very few fragments of painted wall plaster were found (see p. 25), but the walls may have been covered with decorated hangings, as suggested in the picture opposite. Ælfric, monk and grammarian of Old Minster, wrote in his 'Life of Swithun' in the 990s that the church was 'completely hung round, from one end to the other and on either wall with crutches and with the stools of cripples who had been healed there', and these too are indicated on this illustration. The floor was probably paved with flagstones, but the area immediately around the altar may have been covered with tiles, possibly comparable to those which had covered the floor around the altar before the rebuilding of 980 to 992–4 (see pp. 28–9). No furniture of any kind is shown, and there may not have been any at this date.

(left) The interior of the westwork of Old Minster (as dedicated 980) looking west. The shrine of St Swithun, marking the site of his original burial, stands below the tower, in the centre of the ground floor (see pp. 17–18). The first floor, reached by stairs to north and south of the ground floor, may have provided accommodation for a choir or choirs and probably for the king, who could observe the liturgy on the ground floor of the east end of the church. By turning west and moving through an arch at first floor level, the king could appear on a balcony, perhaps on the occasion of public crown-wearings at Easter.

(right) The interior of the nave of Old Minster in its final form as completed 992–4 looking east towards the principal altar beneath the tower.

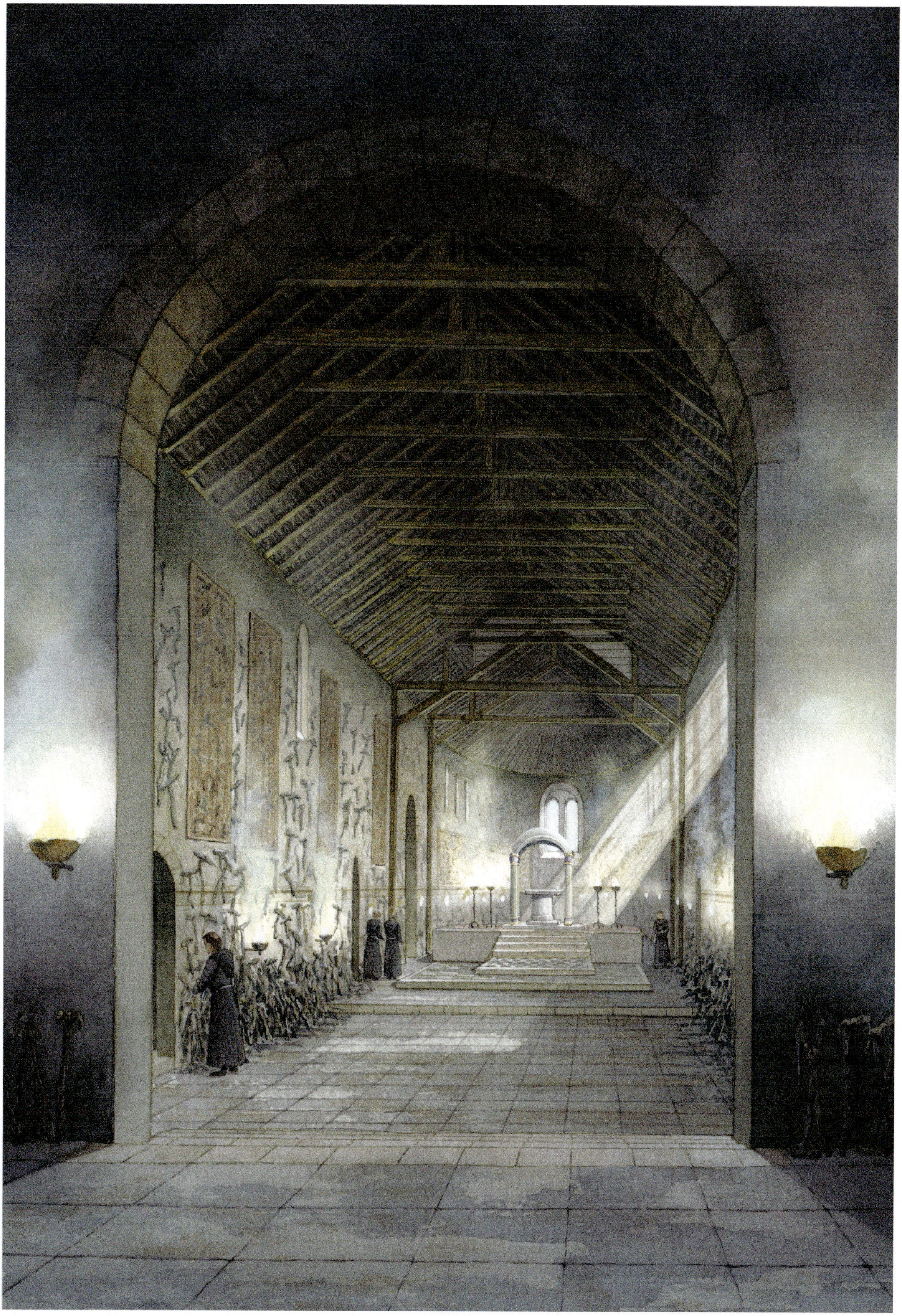

Evolution of Old Minster

Reconstruction of the **Anglo-Saxon Old Minster at Winchester** as completed 992–4

Old Minster was reconstructed to a plan probably devised by Bishop Æthelwold following the translation of St Swithun in 971. Work began on a vast double-apsed martyrium covering the site of the saint's original grave (1a) outside the west door of the seventh century minster (8–10). When the new foundations failed, the structure was rebuilt as a towered rectangular westwork (3–5), dedicated in 980. Æthelwold laid the foundations of the new east end (11–18) but died in 984. His successor Ælfheah completed the works, including the staged timber tower (19–21), which were dedicated in 992–4. By this time the stone coffin in which Swithun had originally been burried in 863 (on the site of 1a) had been moved and placed on the north side of the steps up to the high altar (1b), where the hands of the faithful had worn away the stone of the coffin in which the saint had originally lain.

Key

1a Monument over original grave of St Swithun
1b Original stone coffin of St Swithun
2   High altar of the late 10th-century minster
3   Westwork dedicated in 980
4   South aisle of the upper floor of the westwork
5   South-west tower of the westwork
6   South wing of the early 10th-century façade and chapels
7   Door to the north wing of the early 10th-century façade and chapels
8   Nave of the 7th-century minster
9   South chapel of the 7th-century minster
10 Door to the 7th-century north chapel and baptistery
11 East apse of the late 10th-century minster
12 South apse of the east end dedicated in 992–4
13 Arch to the north apse of the east end dedicated in 992–4
14 Crypt below the high altar of the late 10th-century minster
15 South stairs down to the crypt below the high altar
16 North stairs down to the crypt below the high altar
17 Well in the late 10th-century east end
18 Eastern crypt of the late 10th-century minster
19 Belfry of the late 10th-century minster
20 Copy of the Tomb of Christ covered by a leaded dome
21 The golden weather-cock set on a gilded rod of iron decorated with golden knops
*   The roofs are shingled

Destruction of Old Minster

In November 1066, a month after the Battle of Hastings, the leading citizens of Winchester surrendered their city, going out with gifts to meet their Norman conquerors. Within weeks the Normans had begun to build a castle in the south-west corner of the walled city. From 1068 onwards, every year we know he was in England, William the Conqueror celebrated the Easter feast with a ceremonial wearing of his crown in Old Minster. In the minster on Easter Sunday 1070, William was solemnly recrowned king by the cardinal priests John and Peter, sent by the pope to secure the deposition and imprisonment of the Anglo-Saxon Stigand, simultaneously bishop of Winchester and archbishop of Canterbury. The same year William doubled the size of the old royal palace and began to build a new hall and palace as a setting for his Easter crown-wearings. The new Norman bishop, Walkelin, was consecrated in May that year. The building of a new cathedral began in 1079. The east parts, comprising the choir, crossing, transepts, tower, and first bays of the nave were dedicated on 8 April 1093, the Friday before Palm Sunday, when 'with the greatest exultation and glory ... the monks went from the old minster of Winchester to the new [cathedral] in the presence of all the bishops and

(above) The second coronation of William the Conqueror, in Old Minster on Easter Sunday, 4 April 1070. William, wearing his crown and sitting on a throne with a sceptre in his left hand, is identified by the papal banner (probably that sent by Pope Alexander II), which flies aloft from a staff held in the king's right hand. William is flanked on each side side by a figure with a halo, apparently therefore saints; they perhaps represent the Winchester bishops Swithun and Æthelwold. If the haloes are simply an indication of ecclesiastical status, however – although unusual by this date – the figures might represent (as David Bates has suggested; William the Conqueror (2016), 334–5, Pl. 7) the cardinal-priests, John Minutus of S. Maria in Trastevere, and Peter, perhaps of S. Crisogono, who were sent from Rome by the pope to attend William's coronation. By this interpretation they are seen blessing the king, and each apparently reading from a text on a stand, perhaps the papal mandate.

The drawing is meticulous, laid out with great care within four lightly drawn concentric circles with other arcs perhaps to locate the position of the king's head and of the reading stands in front of the haloed figures. The drawing is not coloured and is on the mostly blank last page of a Winchester manuscript book of benedictions. It gives the impression of a sketch for something much larger, either a hanging or possibly a mural painting. Illustration added in or after 1070 to f. 111r. in the Benedictionale Wintoniense. Paris, BnF, MS. latin. 987. (Courtesy of the Bibliothèque nationale de France, Paris)

abbots of England'. Easter was celebrated on 17 April in the Norman cathedral, but fittingly the shrine of St Swithun was not carried in procession from Old Minster into the new cathedral until his feast on the following 15 July. On Bishop Walkelin's instructions the demolition of Old Minster began the next day and was completed the following year, apart from one *porticus* which was left standing (see illustration on p. 63).

Old Minster lay to the north of the proposed nave of the new cathedral and so was able to remain in use whilst the east end was built. The demolition of Old Minster made way for the building of the new nave and provided some of the stone for its construction, but it was to be another 30 years or so, delayed in part by the collapse in 1107 of the tower over the new crossing, before the nave and towers of the Norman west front were finally complete.

(below) The royal quarter of Winchester in 1093 on the eve of the demolition of Old Minster: the Norman royal palace has been extended over the western part of the New Minster precinct. The eastern part of the Norman cathedral was dedicated on 8 April 1093. Old Minster was demolished during the following year.

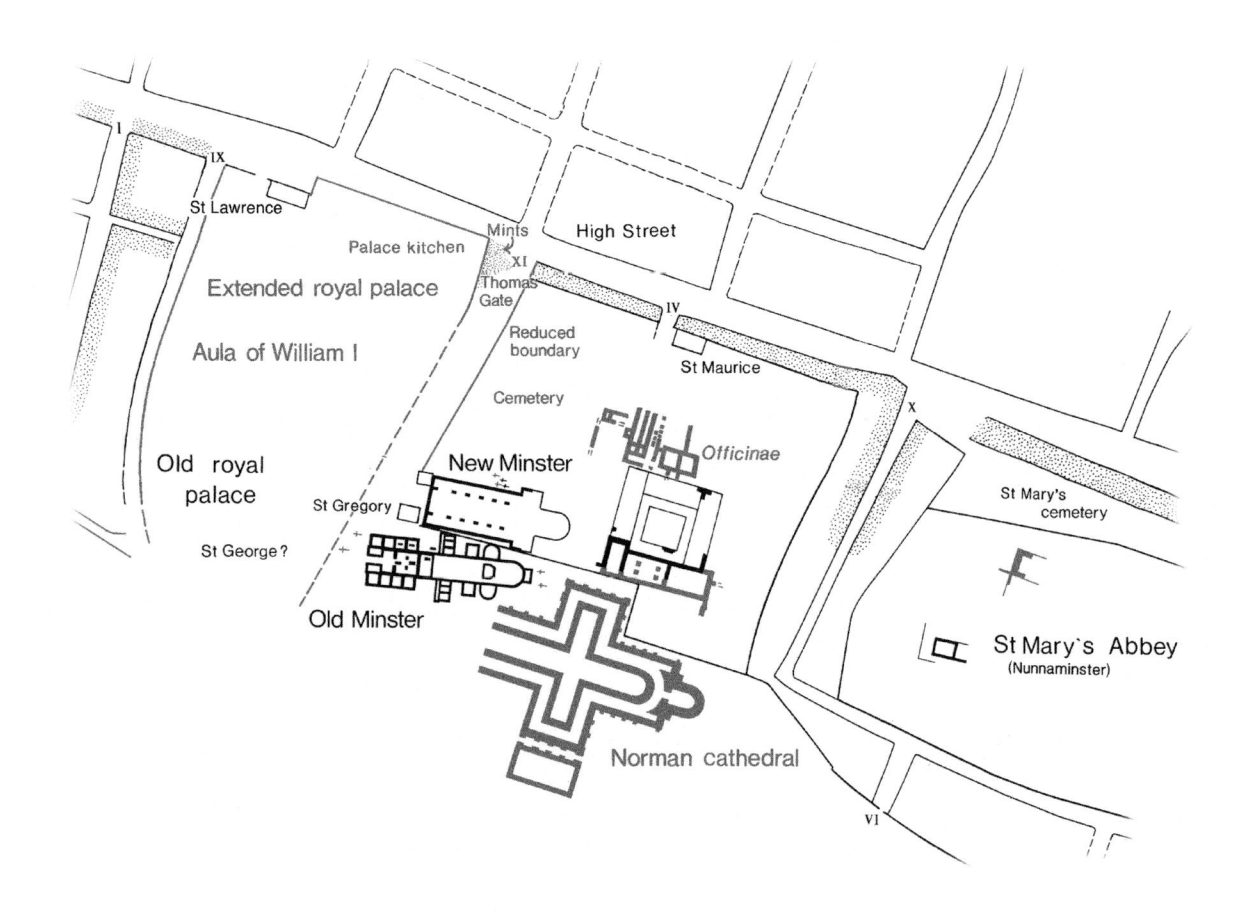

Destruction of Old Minster

The new Norman cathedral was immense: as completed in the 1120s, it was 163 metres long, a little over twice as long as Old Minster, longer when planned in the 1070s than any church in Christendom other than Old St Peter's in Rome. It was, as Eric Fernie has written, a step 'into a different league', perhaps because 'William wanted the building to rival the great cathedrals of the Empire ... a clear statement of [his] wish to be considered in the same light as the German emperors and, at one remove, as Constantine'.

It is at least as likely that the new cathedral represented the legitimacy of William's claim to the English throne through his relationship to Queen Emma, his great-aunt, through her father, and through her brother, Duke Richard II of Normandy (996–1026), William's own grandfather. As New Minster was the burial church of the house of Alfred, erected on the model of Saint-Denis, the burial place of the Merovingian and Carolingian rulers, so Old Minster was the burial church of Cnut and Emma. The bodies of the royal dead were removed from Old Minster in 1093 and placed beside St Swithun in positions of honour around the high altar of the new cathedral. And there they still are today preserved in some sort in the mortuary chests on the choir screens of the cathedral.

William the Conqueror legitimised his rule by coronation in the church at Westminster in which his predecessor Edward the Confessor was buried and Harold had been crowned less than a year before. At Winchester he made concrete his right of succession at the graves of his relatives in the largest church north of the Alps.

It is significant that some features of Old Minster were replicated in the new cathedral. The triple-apsed east end of Old Minster with its long eastern extension is mirrored in the east end of the new church in which, as in the old, the royal burials were placed. And although the new church was on a different alignment, it seems probable that both churches pointed towards some significant feature in the royal palace to the west. The west ends of both churches converged so as to be on almost the same site and to have their west fronts in the form of massive structures, whether the 'westwork' of Old Minster or the twin-towered west front of the Norman cathedral, both appropriate for royal and episcopal appearances at the great feasts of the year, most especially at Easter.

The demolition of Old Minster was completed within a year, except for one chapel (*porticus*) and the high altar, under which 'relics of St Swithun and many other saints' were found. All that remained was a memorial (later enclosed in a small chapel) over the grave of St Swithun, bishop of Winchester from 852–63. The rest of the site of the now vanished Old Minster became known as 'Paradise', and remained until the sixteenth century the principal burial ground of the cathedral.

Soon New Minster was also gone. A fire in 1065 destroyed its domestic buildings, the site of which was taken by William the Conqueror in 1070 to enlarge the site of the ancient royal palace. The monks of New Minster stayed on for forty years, but in 1110 with the support of Henry I they moved to a new site at Hyde outside the north gate, taking with them the bodies of King Alfred, his wife Ealhswith, their son King Edward the Elder, and other children and grandchildren.

Only Nunnaminster remained on its original site. Rebuilt on an immense scale in the early twelfth century, one of the four greatest nunnery churches in medieval England, it was finally dissolved by King Henry VIII in 1539 and almost immediately demolished.

The still standing New Minster (to the left), the site of the demolished Old Minster, and the nave of the new cathedral under construction, looking east about 1120. In the memorial court in the middle foreground, in front of a still standing fragment of Old Minster, a rectangular monument lies over the site of St Swithun's grave (see pp. 16–17), with other important graves in stone coffins still in position around it.

Destruction of Old Minster

The east end of the Norman cathedral and its nave were built on open ground along the south side of Old Minster, in an area which had been the principal cemetery of the minster since its foundation in the middle of the seventh century. Many graves were disturbed in the process: the bones of over a thousand individuals were reburied in the huge hole left by the robbing of the stonework of the deep foundations of the Anglo-Saxon westwork (see pp. 50–1). What remained of the hole after the laying of the massive foundations of the Norman west front (photo opposite) was then filled with bones from the graves (see p. 23).

The vast difference in size between the Anglo-Saxon Old Minster demolished in 1093–4 and the new Norman cathedral built between 1079 and about 1120 (the exact date of its completion and dedication is not recorded) is best seen by comparing the reconstructed outlines of the two buildings as seen from the south and west (picture below). The immense size of the Norman cathedral can best be appreciated today by standing in either the north or south transept; they remain intact as they were built from 1079 onwards and dedicated on their completion in 1093, some 30 years before the nave itself was completed.

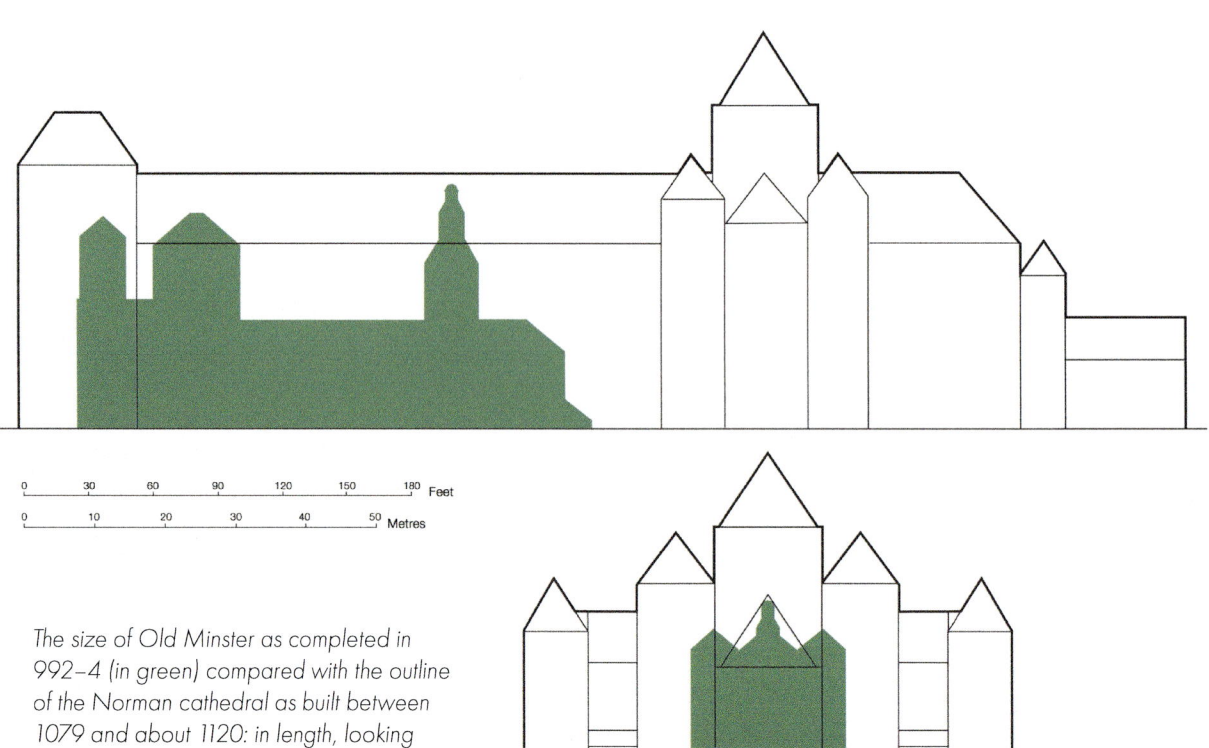

The size of Old Minster as completed in 992–4 (in green) compared with the outline of the Norman cathedral as built between 1079 and about 1120: in length, looking north (above); in width, looking east (right) (see pp. 34–5).

The excavation in 1969 of the north side and north-west corner of the foundations of the west front of the Norman cathedral, in the context of the present, 14th-century, west front.

The Royal Quarter

New Minster

In the late 880s King Alfred of Wessex (871–99) established a *monasteriolum*, 'a little monastery', in Winchester for the distinguished scholar Grimbald whom he had invited to England from the monastery of St Bertin in the Pas-de-Calais. In 901, after Grimbald's death, Alfred's son, Edward the Elder, founded a new monastery immediately north of the Anglo-Saxon cathedral on property which included the site his father had given to Grimbald. This was the New Minster, the *Novum monasterium*, designed to provide a burial church for his father King Alfred, his mother Queen Ealhswith (d. 902), and their dynasty. Two of Edward's sons were buried in his New Minster, and later Edward himself in 924, and King Eadwig in 959.

New Minster extended

King Edmund (939–46) laid new foundations 'at considerable expense', apparently to adorn (presumably to extend) New Minster in memory of his grand-parents and parents who were buried there. He left the work unfinished but 'visible' at his death in 946. The work was completed by his son King Edgar (959–75) and dedicated in 972.

The documents say no more, but in 1970 excavation 30 metres east of the approximate original end of New Minster uncovered part of a massive foundation of layered chalk rubble and flints over a metre thick (see p. 68). Foundations like this were used only once in the long structural history of the neighbouring Old Minster: for the foundation of the building with opposed apses erected in 971–5 around the site of St Swithun's grave (see pp. 48–9).

(above) By the year 1000, Old Minster and New Minster, shown here looking south-east, had both been greatly extended (for Old Minster, see pp. 47–59). In the 970s, New Minster seems to have been enlarged to the east (as hinted by dashed lines to the left on this drawing, see p. 68) and by 988 a six-storey tower covered with sculpture (seen here in the foreground and pictured right) had been added to the New Minster's west front by King Æthelred (978/9–1016).

NEW MINSTER

OLD MINSTER

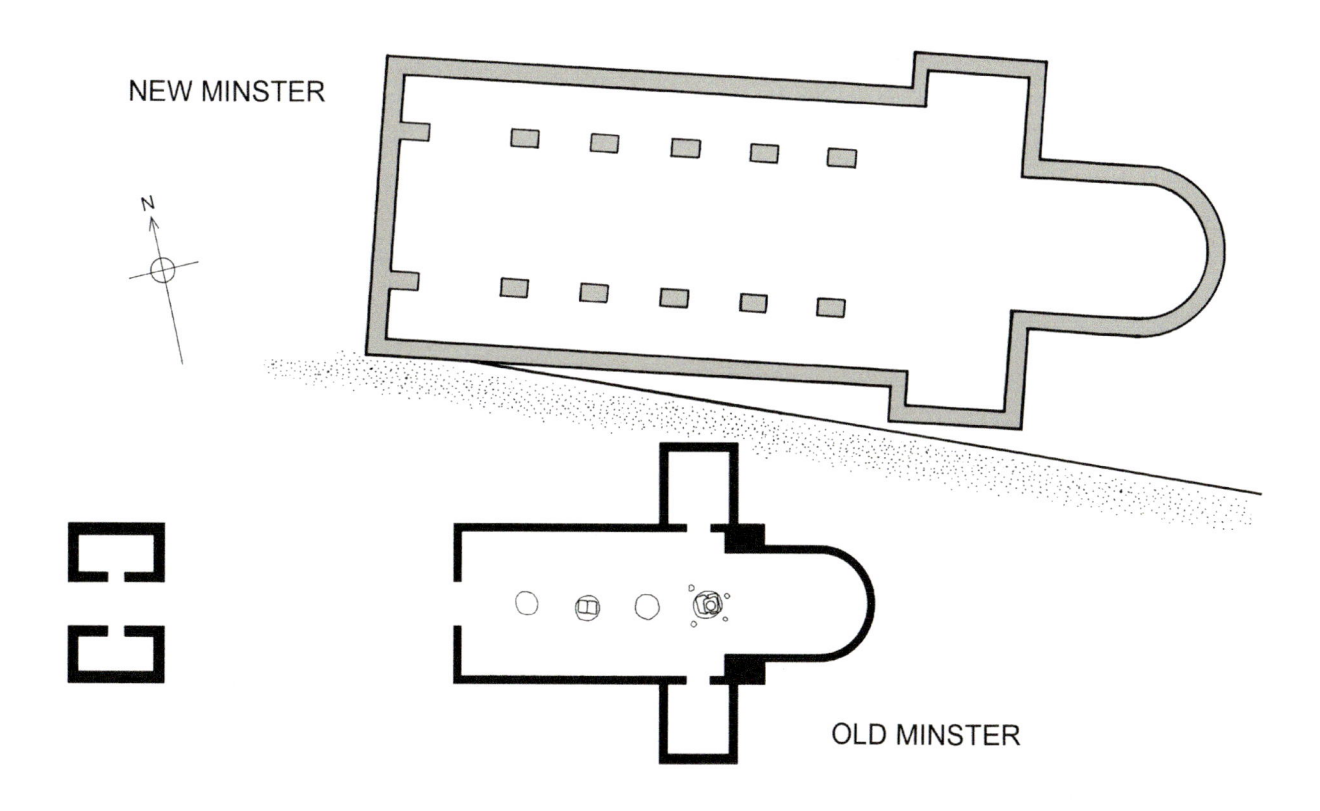

Images on New Minster tower

Each of the six storeys on New Minster's 20-metre high west tower was identified by an external sculpture reflecting its dedication: to the Virgin Mary on the ground floor; the Holy Trinity on the second, the Holy Cross on the third; All Saints on the fourth; the Archangel Michael and all heavenly powers on the fifth; and the Evangelists on the sixth.

(above) In 901–3, King Edward the Elder of Wessex built a large new church with an aisled nave, henceforth New Minster, close alongside the much older and then much smaller cathedral church which later became known as Old Minster. The plan of the new church – an aisled basilica with very shallow transepts – is similar to that of the church which Charlemagne (d. 814) completed at Saint-Denis, afterwards to become the burial church of the kings of France.

The Royal Quarter

If the chalk foundation discovered east of New Minster is also of tenth-century date, it may represent the new foundation laid out by King Edmund in the 940s. If so, New Minster was greatly extended in the mid tenth century to a total length of some 80 metres, making it longer than Old Minster at its greatest extent (see pp. 38–41, 56–9, and 66).

During Cnut's reign the two great minsters of Anglo-Saxon Winchester stood side by side (illustrations on pp. 55 and 66). Cnut gave them equal honour. At an Easter in Winchester he and his wife Emma, widow of King Æthelred, presented a great gold cross for the high altar of New Minster (right).

But disaster was to come: in April 1065 New Minster's domestic buildings were burnt down; the next year Abbot Ælfwig fought against William at Hastings; and by about 1070 the western third or more of the minster's precinct had been taken by William the Conqueror to build a new hall (see p. 69). In 1110, early in the reign of Henry I, the community of New Minster moved to the northern suburb of Hyde, into a new church of majestic proportions, to which they took the bodies of Grimbald and other saints, and their royal dead.

(above) King Cnut and Queen Emma (Ælfgifu) placing a great gold cross on the altar of New Minster, perhaps at Easter 1019. London, BL, MS. Stowe 944, f. 6r. (© The British Library Board)

(right) This massive foundation of carefully laid white chalk found in excavation east of New Minster in 1970 may be part of the extension of the minster by King Edmund in the 940s.

Nunnaminster

By her death in 902 Alfred's widow Ealhswith had acquired a large property inside the east gate of Winchester on the south side of *ceapstræt* ('market street', now The Broadway). Here, perhaps after Alfred's death in 899, she founded a house for women, dedicated to Mary the Mother of God and later known as Nunnaminster (St Mary's Abbey). The dedication of a tower by Archbishop Plegmund about 908 may mark the completion of the buildings. Rebuilt and rededicated in 1108, the minster was one of the four largest nunnery churches in Norman England. Burnt in August 1141 during fighting in the city, the Abbey was rebuilt and continued to flourish with at least 70 nuns up to the early forteenth century. The abbey declined thereafter, although favoured by the citizens and by single women until its dissolution in 1539.

Nunnaminster is the only one of the three Anglo-Saxon minsters of Winchester of which some part can be seen today. Remains of the pre-Conquest church overlain by the vast early Norman nave are displayed alongside Abbey Passage behind the Guildhall.

The Anglo-Saxon and Norman royal palaces

Given the extraordinary importance and scale of the ecclesiastical buildings in the heart of the city, coupled with the honour bestowed upon them by Anglo-Saxon and Norman kings, it seems probable that a royal residence was already present in Winchester in the Anglo-Saxon and Early Norman period.

By the middle of the twelfth century the royal residence was high to the west in the castle where the later Great Hall still stands. But earlier power was exercised from the centre of the city, from the area immediately to the west of the Old and New Minsters, now the cathedral cemetery.

Asser, King Alfred's biographer, writing in 893 asked: 'What of the royal halls and chambers marvellously constructed of stone and wood at his command? And what of the royal residences of masonry … splendidly reconstructed at … appropriate places by his royal command?' One of these stone residences at an appropriate place would have been in Winchester. The earliest written evidence for such a royal residence at Winchester is dated to Pentecost 934 when one of the largest known Anglo-Saxon royal gatherings – 92 persons, including King Athelstan, two archbishops, four Welsh sub-kings, and seventeen bishops – confirmed a grant to one of the king's thegns *in ciuitate opinatissima quae… Winteceaster nuncupatur*, 'in the most renowned city called Winchester'.

In the later 1060s or early 1070s, William the Conqueror extended the site of the residence northwards to build his hall, an indication that the earlier site lay west of Old Minster (see pp. 7, 11, 34, and 61). In a case decided there in 1081 William's residence was described as a *palatium*.

The royal buildings, transferred to Bishop Henry of Blois by 1138, were then perhaps fortified and played a role in the siege of Winchester in 1141. At the end of the twelfth century Gerald the Welshman recalled that the royal houses at Winchester were 'second to those at London in neither quality nor quantity.'

Conclusion

Over the last sixty years, archaeological, documentary, and scientific research in many very varied fields have combined to reveal the origins and changing fortunes of a place that has stood for nearly 2,000 years at a centre of political, social, religious, artistic, and sometimes even economic affairs. The story of the Anglo-Saxon minsters outlined here, although not unsuspected, was in essence unknown six decades ago. A great deal of what has been achieved has been the work of young people from all over the world who took part in the excavations of 1961–71. Research continues to this day and there is much still to be learnt about the origins and buildings of this 'early capital'.

Winchester Studies

Winchester excavations

In 1961 Trust Houses Ltd was about to build a hotel in Winchester on a site then thought to be that of the Anglo-Saxon New Minster. There was at the time in Britain no legal protection for the buried remains of the urban past, which here would have been totally destroyed by the deep basement of what is now the Wessex Hotel. In the event an excavation was arranged with dramatic results: a Roman north–south street flanked to the west by the east range of the forum of *Venta Belgarum* and to the east by a large town house. Over everything were the remains, not of the New Minster church itself, but of part of its cemetery with an oval chapel, and remains of what later became the house of its first Norman abbot, Riwallon from Mont Saint-Michel. The discoveries were so striking that they led in 1962 to the foundation of the Winchester Excavations Committee. Over the next ten years, ending in 1971, the Committee undertook the greatest campaign of research and 'rescue' excavations ever undertaken at the time in an English city. Major excavations took place season after season on the site of Old Minster (the Anglo-Saxon cathedral immediately north of the present cathedral), at the royal castle beside the Great Hall, at the bishop's palace at Wolvesey, and on the medieval town houses and parish churches along and behind Lower Brook Street. Many lesser sites were also investigated in different parts of the city.

Winchester Research Unit

Each year the Committee published an 'interim' report in the journal of the Society of Antiquaries of London – ten reports in all, 399 pages with 145 plates and 94 figures, a permanent initial record of what had been found. But that was clearly not enough.

In September 1966 Martin Biddle and Birthe Kjølbye were invited by Professor Witold Hensel, the director of the Polish Institute for the History of Material Culture, to see the archaeological work being done in Polish towns, each with its own professional team supported by a permanent staff. The visit was a revelation: clearly this had to happen at Winchester if the necessary research and publication were to be possible.

The Winchester Excavations Committee began from the following autumn to develop plans for a permanent research unit. With the support of the Inspectorate of Ancient Monuments, the Winchester Research Unit came into being on 1 October 1968, with financial support from central government, Hampshire County Council, and the City of Winchester.

The excavations themselves continued as before during the summer months of the first three years of the Unit's existence, the final and longest-ever season lasting from May to November 1971. The Winchester Research Unit is not simply an 'Archaeological Unit'. Its unique remit covers written 'historical' evidence for places and persons as well as archaeological evidence in the widest sense of sites and objects, the evidence for human and animal populations, and for the natural environment of plants and insects. The volumes of Winchester Studies, published and in preparation, reflect this approach.

By the end of 2017, eight volumes of Winchester Studies had been published by Oxford University Press. A ninth, the Winchester Historic Towns Atlas, was published by Oxbow books (see p. 72). Three more volumes of Winchester Studies – Prehistoric and Roman Winchester, The Anglo-Saxon Minsters, and Winchester Castle – are approaching completion, and the remainder are in progress.

(left) The Winchester Research Unit staff and volunteers outside the west front of Winchester Cathedral, summer 1976. Between 1968 and 1976 this team (which by the date of this photograph had reached over forty) set about analysis and study of the excavation records and the vast quantities of 'finds', laying the foundations for all the volumes of Winchester Studies, the first of which, Winchester in the Early Middle Ages, was published that autumn. Today the Research Unit operates with only five members, not including a large number of external contributors, many of which are volunteers.

Winchester Studies

The volumes of Winchester Studies so far published cover a wide range of themes, and total 6,565 pages, including 1,340 illustrations, and 480 tables. Seen here (top) are pages from The Cult of St Swithun (WS 4.ii, 2003) by Michael Lapidge, showing the image of St Swithun from a British Library manuscript opposite the title page (see also here p. 8), with a page of the discussion, and (below) pages from Object and Economy (WS 7.ii. 1990), edited by Martin Biddle, which illustrates and discusses over 4,400 objects of Anglo-Saxon and later date found in the excavations of 1961–71.

Winchester Studies

Plans for permanent publication were put in hand. In October 1968 Oxford University Press agreed to publish a series of eleven volumes of Winchester Studies in seventeen parts, under several broad themes (see p. 73). Nine have so far been published, with three more advancing to publication in the next few years (dependent upon funding). The most recent, the *Winchester Historic Towns Atlas*, was published by Oxbow Books in November 2017.

The Winchester Historic Towns Atlas (Winchester Studies 11; Historic Towns Atlas 6) was published by Oxbow Books in November 2017, edited by Martin Biddle and Derek Keene. The base is a map of Winchester about 1800 at a scale of 1:2500, reconstructed (for no map of that period exists) by editing back from the Ordnance Survey 25-inch-to-the-mile survey of 1869–71 and by editing up from William Godson's Plan of Winchester of 1750. Derek Keene (author of Survey of Medieval Winchester, WS 2, 1985), assisted by Fred Aldsworth, then of the Ordnance Survey Continuous Revision Division at Southampton, began work on this in the late 1970s. This base map is published in the Atlas in full colour in nine sheets, accompanied by 17 period and thematic maps, and 13 plates, which reproduce over 100 watercolours, drawings and engravings of the city and of individual buildings dating from the late 16th century to the 1820s. The Atlas includes a text covering all periods of the city's history from the prehistoric to the 20th century, and a gazetteer dealing with all buildings and other features named on the maps.

Winchester Studies

11 studies in 17 volumes (1976–)

WS 1   Martin Biddle (ed.), Winchester in the Early Middle Ages: an edition and discussion of the Winton Domesday (1976)

WS 2   Derek Keene, Survey of Medieval Winchester, 2 vols. (1985)

Pre-Roman and Roman Winchester

WS 3.i   Martin Biddle and Francis Morris, Venta Belgarum: Prehistoric, Roman, and Post-Roman Winchester (in preparation)

WS 3.ii   Giles Clarke, The Roman Cemetery at Lankhills (1979)

The Anglo-Saxon Minsters of Winchester

WS 4.i   Birthe Kjølbye-Biddle and Martin Biddle, The Anglo-Saxon Minsters of Winchester (in preparation)

WS 4.ii   Michael Lapidge, The Cult of St Swithun (2003)

WS 4.iii   Alexander R. Rumble, Property and Piety in Early Medieval Winchester (2002)

Residences and Other Town Sites in Medieval Winchester

WS 5   The Brooks and other Town Sites of Medieval Winchester (in preparation)

WS 6.i   Martin Biddle and Beatrice Clayre, Winchester Castle: Fortress, Palace, Garrison, and County Seat (in preparation)

WS 6.ii   Wolvesey Palace (in preparation)

Artefacts from Medieval Winchester

WS 7.i   Katherine Barclay, Ceramics of Medieval Winchester (in preparation)

WS 7.ii   Martin Biddle, Object and Economy in Medieval Winchester, 2 vols. (1990)

WS 8   Martin Biddle (ed.), The Winchester Mint and Coins and Related Finds from the Excavations of 1961–71 (2012)

Human, Animal and Plant Biology

WS 9.i   Caroline M. Stuckert (ed.), The People of Early Winchester (2017)

WS 9.ii   Mark Maltby, The Animals of Early Winchester (in preparation)

WS 10   Martin Biddle (ed.), Environment, Agriculture, and Gardens in Early Winchester (in preparation)

The Origin and Development of Winchester

WS 11   Martin Biddle and Derek Keene (ed.), Winchester Historic Towns Atlas (2017)

Further Reading
(MB, Martin Biddle; BKB, Birthe Kjølbye-Biddle)

Interim (i.e. provisional) reports on all the sites excavated in Winchester 1961–71 appeared in *The Archaeological Journal* 119 (1962) and in *The Antiquaries Journal* 44 (1964) to 50 (1970), 52 (1972), and 55 (1975).

Illustrated accounts of the excavations beside the cathedral appeared annually in *Winchester Cathedral Record* 31 (1962) to 41 (1972); for Nunnaminster, see 53 (1984).

For the introduction of the metric co-ordinate recording system and of the procedures developed in the excavation of the Anglo-Saxon Old Minster for the recording and interpretation of buildings from robber-trenches, see MB and BKB, 'Metres, Areas and Robbing', *World Archaeology* 1 (1970), 208–19.

For the seventh-century Old Minster and its baptistery, see BKB, 'The 7th-century minster … interpreted', in L. A. S. Butler and R. K. Morris (ed.), *The Anglo-Saxon Church*, CBA Research Report 60 (London, 1986), 196–209, and 'Anglo-Saxon Baptisteries of the 7th and 8th Centuries: Winchester and Repton', in *Acta XIII Congressus Internationalis Archaeologiae Christianae, Split-Poreč 1994* (Vatican City, 1998), ii, 757–78.

For the carved stonework and painted wall-plaster from the minsters, see MB and BKB in *Corpus of Anglo-Saxon Stone Sculpture*, iv, *South-East England* (Oxford, 1995), 96–107, 273–327, Illus. 490–666, 691–4; and in *Early Medieval Wall Painting and Painted Sculpture in England*, BAR Brit. Ser. 216 (Oxford, 1990), 41–71. The window glass, bell foundries and other objects found during the excavation of the minsters, some illustrated in this book, are published in *Object and Economy in Medieval Winchester*, Winchester Studies 7.ii (Oxford, 1990). The coins found are published in *The Winchester Mint*, Winchester Studies 8 (Oxford, 2012), 611–725.

The human remains from the Anglo-Saxon minsters and the overlying cemetery of the Norman and later cathedral were published by T. Molleson et al., in Caroline M. Stuckert (ed.), *The People of Early Winchester*, Winchester Studies 9.i (Oxford, 2017), 261–390. For the problems of excavating, recording and interpreting the medieval cemetery overlying the robbed remains of Old Minster, see BKB in *World Archaeology* 7 (1975), 87–108, and in Steven Bassett (ed.), *Death in Towns* (Leicester, 1992), 234–44.

The final report on the excavation and interpretation of Old Minster, the adjacent parts of New Minster, and the later cemetery with the chapel of St Swithun is in preparation: †BKB and MB, *The Anglo-Saxon Minsters of Winchester*, Winchester Studies 4.i.

For Eric Fernie's discussion of the Norman Cathedral (quoted on p. 62) see Fernie, E., *The Architecture of Norman England* (Oxford, 2000), 117–21.